Playing to Learn
Activities and Experiences that Build Learning Connections

Carol Seefeldt

Illustrations by Katheryn Davis

Dedication

This book is dedicated to Head Start, the program that gave me my start.

Acknowledgments

I would like to acknowledge the continual support and guidance of
Dr. Alice Galper, my friend, and Kathy Charner, my editor.
In addition, I would like to thank Nancy Goldsmith for her editing work,
Karheryn Davis for her wonderful illustrations, the people who reviewed the book,
and all the Gryphon House staff for helping to create this book.

Playing TO LEARN

Carol Seefeldt

gryphon house®, inc.
Beltsville, Maryland

Library of Congress Cataloging-in-Publication Data

Seefeldt, Carol.
    Playing to learn: activities and experiences that build learning connections /Carol Seefeldt; illustrations by Katheryn Davis.
        p. cm.
    Includes bibliographical references and index.
    ISBN 0-87659-263-9
        1. Play. 2. Early childhood education—Curricula. 3. Learning. 4. Child development.
    I. Title.
    LB1139.35.P55 S44 2001
    372.13--dc21

                                                                2001023957

Cover photograph: Ariel Skelley, Corbis Stock Market © 2001
Illustrations: Katheryn Davis

Bulk purchase

Gryphon House books are available at special discount when purchased in bulk for special premiums and sales promotions as well as for fund-raising use. Special editions or book excerpts also can be created to specification. For details, contact the Director of Sales at the address above.

Disclaimer

The publisher and the author cannot be held responsible for injury, mishap, or damages incurred during the use of or because of the activities in this book. The author recommends appropriate and reasonable supervision at all times based on the age and capability of each child.

Table of Contents

INTRODUCTION

The Author's Philosophy 9
  Age-Appropriate 9
  Goal-Directed .10
  Integrated 10
  Continuous 10
  Language-Filled 10
  Social 10
What You Will Need 10
  Goals 10
  Centers of Interest 11
Knowledge of Age Appropriateness 11
  Two-Year-Olds 11
  Three-Year-Olds 11
  Four-Year-Olds 11
  Five-Year-Olds 11
Tools You'll Find Useful 12
  Books 12
  Clipboards 12
  Making Books 13
    Fostering Invented Spelling 13
Assessing and Evaluating 14
How to Get Started 14

CHAPTER 1
Playing to Learn on a Wet and Rainy Day

Physical Activities for Active Children 16
  Jacks and Jills in Boxes 17
  Jumping Jacks and Jills 17
  Jacks and Jills on Hills 18
  Jacks and Jills and Candlesticks 19
  A Sun Beam Walk 22
  Sun Beams on Display 23
Moving All Around 24
  Rainy Day Play 24
  Balloon Play .24
  Train Play 25
  Hoop Play 26
  Hollow Block Play 26
Thinking Children: Time to Study, Think,
  and Learn 28
  Measure Rain .28
  What Rain Does 30

  Rain Changes What You Wear 31
  Rainy Day Clothes Are Different 31
  Which One Dries Faster? 32
  Rain Changes the Environment 33
  What Are the Properties of Rain? 33
  How Does Rain Change Soil? 34
Artistic Children 35
  Watercolors 35
Literate Children 36
  April Rain Song 36
  Finally, Rain! .36
  Are You Crying? 37
  A Rainy Day Poem 37
  Rain Song 37
  Rainy Day Books 38
Quiet Children 39
  Listening to the Rain 39
  Collect My Thoughts 39
Assessing and Evaluating Children Playing to Learn
  on a Wet and Rainy Day 41

CHAPTER 2
Playing to Learn on a Hot and Sunny Day

Planning and Reflecting Children 44
  Making Plans .45
  Books 45
  Reflection 46
  Plan for Hydration 46
  Our Own Drinks 47
  Juicers 48
  Summarize and Reflect 49
  Frosty Chocolate Milk 49
  Make Yourself Some Shade 50
Artistic Children 51
  About Hats 51
  Making Hats .51
  Decorating Hats 52
Children Are Physical Scientists 53
  Shadows 53
  Props and Shadows 53
  Hand Shadows 54
  Dissolving 54
  Melting 55

What Else Melts? 55
Water Words 56
Water Math 56
Water Measuring 57
Water Graphing 57
Cooperating 58
Just Having Fun 58
Basic Water Play 59
Plastic Squirt Bottles 59
Sparkling Clean 60
Wet and Dry Reflections 60
Paint the World 61
Go Fish 61
Mud Pies .61
Children Experience Language 62
Too Hot to Move 62
Cool Poetry 63
Tales About the Sun 63
Assessing and Evaluating Children Playing To
Learn on a Hot and Sunny Day 64

CHAPTER 3
Playing to Learn on a Windy Day
Observing Children 66
The Effects of the Wind 66
The Wind .67
Blowing Wind 68
Wind Experiment 68
Clouds 69
Clouds Are Different 70
It Looked Like... 71
Predicting the Weather 71
Catch the Wind with Parachutes 72
Observing Parachutes 73
Reading About Wind 73
Wind and Water 74
Which Way Does the Wind Move? 74
Catch the Wind with Kites 75
Making Kites 75
Reflecting on Wind and Kites 76
Kites in Different Cultures 76
Paper Airplanes 77
Just Seeds in the Wind 78
Wind Toys 78
Wind Bag .79
Catch the Wind with Bubbles 79
Feel the Force of the Wind 79
Windstorms 80

Listening Children 80
The Sounds of the Wind 80
Do You Hear the Wind Singing? 81
Describe the Wind 81
Wind Instruments 82
Assessing and Evaluating Children Playing to Learn
on a Windy Day 83

CHAPTER 4
Playing to Learn on a Perfectly Beautiful Day
Types of Play 86
Exploratory Play 86
Constructive Play 86
Dramatic Play 86
Games With Rules 87
Exploring Children 87
Toddlers and Boxes 87
Toddlers and Cars 88
Toddlers and Dump and Fill 88
Toddlers and Pull Toys 88
Toddlers, Boxes, and Blocks 89
Toddlers and Dumping 89
Toddlers and Tubes 89
Toddlers and Bracelets 90
Toddlers and Sand 90
Preschoolers and Tunnels 90
Preschoolers Finding Out How Things Work .91
Put It Together and Take It Apart 91
Preschoolers and Magnifiers 92
Exploring Sand 92
Constructive Children 94
Boards and Wooden Boxes 94
Building Structures 95
Junk and Boxes 96
Outside Clay 96
Outside Fingerpaint 97
Outside Painting 97
Dramatic and Cooperative Children 98
Wheel Toys 98
Work Props 99
Field Trip to Stimulate Dramatic Play 99
Housekeeping Play 100
Children Play Games With Rules 100
Circle Games for Children Under Three 100
Skill Games for Children Under Three 101
Circle Games for Threes and Young Fours . .102
Circle Games for Older Fours and Fives 103
Chasing Games for Older Fours and Fives . .105

Games of Skill for Older Fours and Fives 105
Children Play With Language to End a Perfectly
    Beautiful Day .107
    Funny, Silly Poems and Stories 107
Assessing and Evaluating Children Learning to Play
    on a Perfectly Beautiful Day 108

CHAPTER 5
Playing to Learn When You Have to Wait

Involving Children 110
Giving Time 110
Literate Children 110
    Poetry Bag 111
    ABC Bag 111
    Name Bag 112
    Poems for Naptime 113
    Poems for Cleanup Time 114
    Poems for Lunch or Snack 114
    Enchanting Sounds 115
Mathematical Children 116
    Measurement Game—Big-Little 117
    Measurement Game—Unit Blocks 117
    Measurement Books 118
    Number Sense and Numeration—Mystery Bag 119
    Number Sense and Numeration—Count the Children . .119
    Number Sense and Numeration—Count the Moves . . .120
    Number Sense and Numeration—A Counting Game . .120
    Number Sense and Numeration—Japanese Folk Game .121
    Number Sense and Numeration—Fingerplays 121
    Geometry and Spatial Sense—I Spy 123
    Geometry and Spatial Sense—Books 124
    Geometry and Spatial Sense—Mystery Bag 124
    Estimation 125
Laughing, Joyous Children 125
    Reading Silly Books 125
    Play Silly Games—Keep the Basket Full 126
    Play Silly Games—Rag Dolls 126
    Play Silly Games—Wiggle Game 126
    Play Silly Games—A Tapping Game 127
    Sing Silly Songs and Chants 127
Assessing and Evaluating Children Learning to Play
    When They Have to Wait 128

CHAPTER 6
Playing to Learn When Things Go Wrong

Children Make Transitions 131
    When School Begins 132
    Transitioning to School 133
    Say Hello 133
    Make a Welcome Chart 134
    Saying Good-Bye 134
    Friends Book 135
    Good-Bye Book .136
Children Make and Keep Friends 136
    Helping Children Make Friends 136
    Highlight the Skills of Children 137
    Guiding Children 137
    Sock Puppets 138
    Books About Social Skills 138
Guiding Children's Behaviors When Groups
    Get Out of Hand .140
    Speak Softly 140
    A Change of Pace 140
    Turn It Off! 141
    Take a Break 141
    Quiet Activities 142
    Analyze What Happened 142
Guiding Children's Behaviors When Children
    Need Help 143
    Helping Children Gain Control 143
    Helping Aggressive Children 143
    Observing an Aggressive Child 144
    Working With an Aggressive Child 144
Children Cope With Life Events 145
    Stay Calm 145
    Keep Daily Routines the Same 145
    Minimize Stress .146
    Observing and Listening to Children 146
    Preparing for Discussion, Play, and Action . .146
Assessing and Evaluating Children Learning to Play
    When Things Go Wrong 148

CHAPTER 7
Playing to Learn When You Take a Walk

Observing Children 150
    Developing Observation Skills 151
    Animals' Eyes 151
    Look and Magnify 152
    Viewing Tubes 152
    A Circle of Yarn .153
    Start with the Familiar 154
    Observing Shapes 154
    Observing People 154
    Observing Older Children 155
    Observing Details 155

Observing Machines 156
A Studying Walk 156
Observing by Listening 157
Listening Game 157
Guess What Is Inside 158
Listening Walks 158
Read and Walk 159
Sing and Walk 159
Walks Around the Neighborhood 160
More Ideas for Listening Walks 160
A Map of Our World 161
Broadening Children's Horizons 161
Children's Social and Physical World 163
Children's Social World 163
Children's Physical World 164
Children's Economic World 164
Shopping Trips 165
Trip to Pick Apples or Pumpkins 166
Assessing and Evaluating Children Playing to
Learn When Taking a Walk 167

CHAPTER 8
Playing to Learn on a Birthday
Before Beginning Birthday Celebrations 170
Mathematical Children 171
Birthday Crown 171
Your Birthday Number 172
Count the Days 172
Calendar Counting 172
Decorate the Cake 173
Birthday Chart 174
Literate Children 174
Growing Up 174
A Birthday Book 175
Books for Older Children 175
Birthday Cards 177
Make Your Own Post Office 177
Learning Letters 178
Growing Children 179
Talk About Growing 179
Guess Who? .179
Birthdays in the Past 180
Musical Children 181
Songs and Music 181
Marching Birthday Band 182
Mathematical Marching 182
Time to Rest 183
Birthday Fun and Games 183
I Made Ice Cream! 183

What Did We Learn? 184
Books About Ice Cream 184
Party Games 185
Assessing and Evaluating Children Playing to
Learn on a Birthday 186

REFERENCES **187**
Books for Children 187
Books and Articles for Teachers 190

INDEX **191**

Introduction

Designed for teachers of children between the ages of two through five, *Playing to Learn* is an encyclopedia of experiences that engage children in learning. Teachers of young children are very busy people who welcome resources that will enable them to become more effective. The variety of learning experiences in this book offers teachers ideas for involving children's hands and minds through play on a:

★ Wet and Rainy Day
★ Hot and Sunny Day
★ Windy Day
★ Perfectly Beautiful Day
★ Day When You Have to Wait
★ Day When Things Go Wrong
★ Day When You Take a Walk
★ Birthday

Playing to Learn includes suggestions for adapting activities to meet the requirements of children with special needs. In addition, ideas for connecting home and school are provided in each of the chapters. Through parents' involvement, books and other children's literature, and specific experiences, children will recognize, respect, and value multiple cultures (Seefeldt & Galper, 2001).

The Author's Philosophy

This book is based on the philosophy that children learn through meaningful, first-hand, interesting experiences (Dewey, 1944; Piaget & Inhelder, 1969). Rather than presenting a list of isolated activities that may keep children busy for a few moments but teach nothing, this book presents meaningful experiences that engage children in learning through play. The experiences do so because they are age-appropriate, goal-directed, integrated, continuous, language-filled, and social.

Age-Appropriate

All the activities in this book are age-appropriate and are based on the knowledge and research of children's cognitive, physical, social, and emotional development (Bredekamp & Copple, 1997).

While the activities respect and value the childish nature of children, none of the experiences denigrate children. Children are not asked to engage in meaningless activities, such as pasting popcorn on paper to make a picture of "snow" or cutting out patterns of bunnies for a display. Rather, the experiences are designed to match children's learning and development and, at the same time, challenge them to new and better ways of thinking (Bredekamp & Copple, 1997).

9

Goal-Directed

The experiences are planned and organized around specific learning goals. These stem from the national standards in specific content discipline areas as well as from position papers from the National Association for the Education of Young Children and those of the Association for Childhood Education International. This grounding in standards gives the experiences meaning and integrity (Bredekamp & Rosegrant, 1995).

Integrated

Learning experiences are not isolated, one-shot occurrences. Rather, they are integrated through play. Content and ideas from mathematics, the sciences, arts, and the language arts are integrated throughout the experiences.

Continuous

Learning experiences also are continuous. One play activity builds on another to form a meaningful, continuous whole. In addition, the home-school connections suggested in the book foster continuity of learning from the child care or preschool setting to the home (Dewey, 1944).

Language-Filled

Each of the play experiences involves children in language learning. Many revolve around children listening to stories, poetry, chants, or songs. Others focus on listening and speaking, writing, and reading (Piaget & Inhelder, 1969).

Social

The experiences are based on the philosophy that learning is a social affair (Vygotsky, 1986). Children learn as they work and play with others (Seefeldt, 1993).

Experiences from a variety of cultures are included and specific books about African American, Hispanic, Asian, and other cultures are suggested throughout to extend and expand children's multicultural learning.

The social context of learning also involves learning for children with special needs. Their inclusion is fostered through a number of experiences.

What You Will Need

While the experiences in this book do not require any special equipment or materials, they do require a developmentally appropriate classroom. To use the experiences in this book to foster children's learning, you will need goals and centers of interest.

Goals

Your program's goals and objectives will guide you in selecting experiences that will be productive for the children you work with.

Centers of Interest

All good centers for young children arrange both in- and outdoor spaces through centers of interest. Centers are clearly delineated spaces organized around a theme or content area. A typical child care center or preschool setting will have a:

★ socio-dramatic play area
★ library and book area
★ art area
★ computer/listening/media center
★ game and manipulative/mathematics area
★ block center
★ science areas
★ music area
★ private spaces for rest, relaxation, and reflection

Knowledge of Age Appropriateness

Knowledge of normal growth and development is necessary in order to select appropriate learning experiences from this book.

Two-Year-Olds

When selecting play experiences for two-year-olds, use only those that involve the children in play and sensori-motor activities. Read and sing to individuals or to small groups of two or three children. Informally and individually, introduce them to new ideas and materials. The play of two-year-olds is primarily parallel in nature.

Three-Year-Olds

Three-year-olds also learn best through play and sensori-motor experiences. However, they are becoming more social than two-year-olds and will be able to participate for short periods of time listening to stories, playing games, or playing along side each other (associative play).

Four-Year-Olds

Four-year-olds are moving from associative play to playing cooperatively with each other. They can listen to learn about their world and enjoy group activities. Their high energy level demands experiences that involve them physically as well as mentally.

Five-Year-Olds

Five-year-olds can work and play cooperatively, make plans as a group, and negotiate with each other to carry out the plans. Therefore, they are ready for a variety of challenging learning experiences. Their increasing ability to use and learn through symbols makes them ready for beginning writing and reading experiences.

12

Tools You'll Find Useful

Books

You will need a wide variety of children's literature, including books, poetry, finger-plays, rhymes, music, and chants. Suggestions are included. If you do not have these specific books in your library, contact your local librarian and ask him or her to order them for you.

It is not necessary to have the exact recommended book or poem to carry out the experience. The suggested books were chosen because they extend children's experiences, introduce specific content, or reflect differing cultural views. You can find similar books on web sites, your local library's web page, or in your own library. See pages 187-190 for complete information on all suggested books.

Clipboards

Many of the activities call for clipboards and markers. Two-year-olds simply enjoy carrying these around and making random marks or scribbles on the attached paper as they play. Three-year-olds can use clipboards either to scribble or write as they play or for more serious work. For example, children might use clipboards to record snack food preferences or note when they've finished their snack.

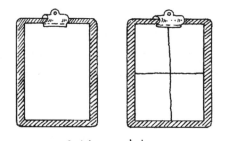

3-Year-olds

You can ask four- and five-year-olds to use clipboards to record all types of information, as well as take notes on a field trip or walk. Clipboards are also recommended for informal use as children use them to write or sketch their observations or record a thought (Seefeldt, 1995).

4-5-Year-olds

Making Books

Throughout this book, suggestions are given for making books. One type of book is for individuals to make. This type of book consists of a couple of pieces of blank newsprint stapled between two sheets of colored construction paper. Keep a supply of these books in the writing area for children to use at any time.

Another type of book is a group book. For this book, children will have had a common experience or purpose. Each child will contribute a page to the book by drawing, writing, or dictating his ideas. Staple together the individual pages between two pieces of tag board to form a book. Or, use a hole punch and join the book with rings.

Some teachers enjoy cutting paper to make special books. For example, make a rainy day book by cutting paper in the form of a raindrop, or cut a circle to represent the sun for a sunny day book.

Fostering Invented Spelling

Throughout the book, you will also find directions for children to draw/write because children naturally move from scribbling to drawing and writing using invented spelling. Scribbling occurs in two phases: 1) random, uncontrolled scribbles; and 2) controlled scribbling in which children gradually scribble objects they can name and which others can recognize.

Around the age of four or five, schemas begin to appear in children's scribbles. Children now use schemas, such as a circle and stick legs to represent a person or a rectangle with a triangle on the top for a house.

Early on, as children scribble, they will incorporate pretend writing into their work. They will use random letter-like forms to represent writing. By the age of four or five, children will "read" their writing to you (for example, "This says, 'I love you.' "). They will also ask you how to spell a given word or ask, "Is this right?"

Asking children to say the word and then write it enables them to make hypotheses about letter-sound correspondence. By forming their own hypotheses about how words sound and are written, they are better able to learn conventional spelling and writing.

In addition to asking children to draw or write, there are times where taking dictation is recommended. By asking children to tell you what they want to say and writing it as they say it, children learn that what they think can be said, what they say can be written, and that others can read and gain meaning from the writing.

Asking children to dictate from time to time also gives them a model to follow. This may be especially useful for children of different cultures whose home language does not use the alphabetic principle.

Assessing and Evaluating

Each chapter ends with a web of concepts, skills, and ideas that children have experienced. Use this web as a model to develop your own web of concepts and skills that children gained after their experiences. Duplicate the web and send it home to parents so they can see what their children are doing and learning in your program.

You could also use the web as a template for observing and recording children's growth and learning. After you chart the ideas, skills, or concepts children experienced, observe individuals over a week during free play and work time. Note any time that they use vocabulary found in a book, apply a mathematical skill, spontaneously sing a song, help another child, and so on. Over time, these observations will give you a picture of an individual child's growth, learning, and development.

Keeping samples of children's work that they completed as a part of the experiences is another way to determine how children are progressing. Another way of developing a clear picture of how children are doing is to keep samples of artwork and invented spelling, records of how they solved problems, and photos of them working together (Seefeldt & Galper, 1998). Label each piece of work with the date and a note containing what the child said about the work, what the child did, or why the work is important and keep them in a portfolio.

How to Get Started

Take a few minutes to scan the experiences in each of the eight chapters. You'll find that they offer children content from every discipline: social science, art, dance and music, the biological and physical sciences, health, safety and nutrition, and language arts. Together the experiences foster children's emotional, social, intellectual and physical learning, growth, and development.

By scanning the book, you may find a rainy day activity that fits very well on any other day, or an activity suggested for a beautiful day that is perfect for a day when everything goes wrong. Reading through the book will also spur your own thinking and creativity as you come across other play experiences that you can adapt, change, expand, or extend to make them more meaningful for the children you teach.

Whether it is rainy or sunny or any other day, just select one of the many play experiences in this book. When you select play ideas that meet children's developmental level, interests, and needs, and fulfill your program's goals, you and the children are sure to have a lot of fun and enjoyment. I've used each of the play experiences as a teacher of young children, and I'm certain you'll find each to be as packed with fun, joy, laughter, and learning as I have.

CHAPTER 1

Playing to Learn on a Wet and Rainy Day

"Rain, rain, go away. We want to go outside to play," sing the children

on a wet and rainy day. Playing outside is where children want to be.

After all, when they're outside, they're free to run, jump, yell, and really be children.

But rainy days, or any other day that children must stay inside, can still be fun-filled,

enjoyable, learning days. That is, if you've planned ahead and are

ready with challenging, engaging learning experiences that include:

★ *physical activity*

★ *time to study, think, and learn*

★ *art and music*

★ *plenty of literature*

★ *quiet times for rest, reflection, and contemplation*

This chapter includes many play activities and experiences.

(Far too many to use on any given day, rainy or not!) Read over the ideas and select those that

best meet the needs of the children you teach. Some of the ideas require advance planning.

You can plan ahead by collecting the materials needed for a given activity and placing them

in a discarded shoebox or other container. Label the container and pull it out

on a rainy day, or any other day.

Physical Activities for Active Children

Children are physically active. They can't keep their rapidly growing energetic bodies still for very long.

They simply must be able to wiggle, jiggle, move, jump, and run —

and they'll do so whether you want them to or not! So on a rainy day,

plan all kinds of physical activities.

When the noise level starts to rise in the room, and the children's voices start to sound whiney, anxious,

and tense, and you can see and feel their frustration mounting, stop the children and

tell them it's time for the following activities.

Jacks and Jills in Boxes

Materials
Jack-in-the-Box toy

Gather the children together on the story or music rug.
Show them a Jack-in-the-Box.
Chant:
Jack is quiet down in his box
Until someone opens the lid.

Pause for a while, with suspense, and then say loudly,

"POP!"

Repeat the chant, substituting the name Jill in place of Jack.
Now ask the children to find a space in the room that's all their own.
(Show them how to do this by standing still and holding out their arms. If their arms do not
touch another child's, they have their own space.)
Tell them to pretend to be Jack or Jill all folded up inside a box.
Chant the verse. To add suspense and tension, pause for a while before saying,
"POP!" When you say, "POP!" all the children jump out of their "boxes."

Jumping Jacks and Jills

Materials
Drum, optional

Are the children still full of wiggles? Ask them to go back to their own space
and pretend to be jumping jacks.
Begin by asking them to jump up and down.
Beat on a drum, following their jumping patterns.
Then ask them to:
★ jump high, landing softly
★ jump low, landing lightly
★ develop a pattern for jumping high, then low, then high again
★ jump in different directions, landing lightly each time
End the activity by leading them with drumbeats and asking them to follow the beat: jumping
quickly, slowly, loudly, and softly.

Jacks and Jills on Hills

Materials
None needed

Ask the children if they know any other poem or verse about Jack and Jill. If they don't respond, then chant all the verses of "Jack and Jill."

*Jack and Jill went up a hill
To fetch a pail of water.
Jack fell down and broke his crown,
And Jill came tumbling after.*

*Then up Jack got,
And home did trot,
As fast as he could caper;
To old Dame Dob
Who patched his nob,
With vinegar and brown paper.*

*When Jill came in,
How she did grin
To see Jack's paper plaster;
Her mother, vexed,
Did beat her next,
For laughing at Jack's disaster.*

*Now Jack did laugh
And Jill did cry,
But her tears did soon abate;
Then Jill did say,
That they should play
At seesaw across the gate.*

Ask the children if they would rather be Jack or Jill.
After they have decided, reread the first stanza and encourage the children
to pretend to be either Jack or Jill. (Beforehand, ask them to plan how they will
fall down the hill in the classroom so they won't hurt themselves.)
Continue reading the first stanza until the children tire.
If they show interest, encourage them to act out the rest of the story.

Jacks and Jills and Candlesticks

Materials

Art materials

Say the following nursery rhyme:

Jack be nimble,
Jack be quick,
Jack jump over the candlestick.

Repeat the rhyme, substituting Jill in place of Jack.
Ask the children to pretend to be either Jack or Jill and jump over
a pretend candlestick as you recite the verse.
Do they want to pretend more? Ask them to describe their candle. What color is it? How big is
it? Does it have any decorations? What kind? Does it have a lovely smell or is it unscented?
Then role-play the rhyme again.

Are the children all settled down by now? Recite all three rhymes again.
Give them art materials, such as paper, markers, easel paints, clay, or playdough, and ask them to
pick one of the following Jacks and Jills to draw, paint, or model from clay: the ones in the box,
the ones going up the hill, or the ones jumping over the candlestick.
Make a class mural of the children's drawings. Label it "Jacks and Jills" and print the appropriate
rhyme under the pictures.

Connecting Home and School

Make the home-school connection
by copying the Jack and Jill poems
(see page 21). Send them home along with a note
(see sample on the following page) explaining the
children's interactions with the poems and the value
of the poems to children's auditory memory,
development of large muscle control, knowledge of
rhyming words, beginning reading and
writing skills, and so on.

Sample Note to Parents

Dear Families,

Your children have enjoyed learning Jack and Jill poems. Here is a copy of the poems for you and your children to enjoy together. Read them with your children. You may want to encourage them to show you how they played with the poem, or ask them to fill in the rhyming words or phrases.

While your children were playing games with these poems, they were learning the necessary beginning reading skills of:

★ *rhyming words—which leads to identification of word families*

★ *auditory memory—remembering the sounds of letters, which is necessary for future reading*

★ *phoneme awareness—learning the beginning sounds of letters*

★ *print awareness—learning that what they say can be written down in print, and what is printed can be read*

★ *vocabulary and concepts—such as lightly, softly, tumbling, and so on*

Thank you for your continuing interest in your children's learning through play.

Sincerely,

The Jack and Jill poems:

Jack Be Nimble
Jack be nimble,
Jack be quick,
Jack jump over the candlestick.

Jack and Jill
Jack and Jill went up a hill
To fetch a pail of water.
Jack fell down and broke his crown,
And Jill came tumbling after.

Then up Jack got,
And home did trot,
As fast as he could caper;
To old Dame Dob
Who patched his nob,
With vinegar and brown paper.

When Jill came in,
How she did grin
To see Jack's paper plaster;
Her mother, vexed,
Did beat her next,
For laughing at Jack's disaster.

Now Jack did laugh
And Jill did cry,
But her tears did soon abate;
Then Jill did say,
That they should play
At seesaw across the gate.

Quiet Jack
Jack is quiet down in his box
Until someone opens the lid.
POP!

A Sun Beam Walk

Materials
Masking or electrical tape

By now a sun beam or two would help!
Make Sun Beam Walks using masking or electrical tape.
Tape two 6' (2 m) strips of tape to the floor, about 8' (2.5 m) apart.
These are the "sun beams" or balance beams.
You need more than one "sun beam" so children won't have to wait as long for their turn. You may even have room for three beams.
Start by asking the children to take turns walking on the beam.

It's surprising how much balance is required simply to walk on the beam!
After the children have played around with the beams, introduce some challenges:
★ Heel to Toe—Show the children how to walk on the beam with their heel touching their toe.
★ Butterfly Walk—Ask the children to walk on the beam as a butterfly would, slowly moving their arms up and down like butterfly wings.
★ Backward Walk—Encourage them to try walking backwards on the beam.
★ Tiptoe Walk—How does it feel to walk tiptoe on the beam?

Sun Beams on Display

Materials
Camera and film
Colored construction paper
Tape or glue
Brown wrapping paper
Markers
Shiny paper or ribbon, optional

Take photographs of the children walking on the "sun beams."
After you get the photos developed, the children may want to sort through them,
pulling out their own photo or those of their friends.
After the children have enjoyed looking at the photos, make a display for the hallway.
Tape or glue the photos onto colored construction paper.
Then tape the construction paper on a strip of brown wrapping paper.
Title it, "Walking on a Sun Beam."
Label each photo with the children's names.
If desired, create a "sun beam" using shiny paper or ribbon to pull the display together.

Connecting Home and School

Copy the photographs to send
home to parents so they can see
their children walking on a "sun
beam."

Moving All Around

When children seem filled with physical energy (especially late in the day),
here are some ways of connecting their physical energy with their creative energy.

Rainy Day Play

Materials
Rain Song by Lezlie Evans

Read *Rain Song* by Lezlie Evans to the children. The children in this book recreate a rain dance to the beat of a drum. They beat on a drum as the lightening flashes, "big, boom, bashing," and dance to the beat of the drum in time with the rain until the rain slows and the thunder stops. After you read the book, ask the children to recreate the sounds of the rain with drums and other rhythm instruments as they dance to the rain.

Balloon Play

Materials
Large balloons
Short pieces of string
Music

Blow up a few large balloons, enough for each child to have at least one.
Tie a piece of string to each balloon.
Give the balloons to the children and encourage them to dance and play with them.
The balloons will float in the air when the children tap them.
Or they can simply trail the balloons behind them, holding onto the string.
Follow the children's graceful motions with music. Play some chords on the piano or autoharp, or just sing or hum a tune in time to their motions.

Train Play

Materials
Hula-hoops, or loops of cloth
Piano or guitar, optional

Do you have some old hula-hoops? If not, make some by making loops
out of stretching cloth or other material.
Assign children various "train" roles: a conductor, engineer, engine,
passenger cars, freight cars, and caboose.
Play "chug-chug" music on the piano or guitar, or just chant a "chug-chug" sound.
Ask each child to place a hoop around her middle. The children will form a "train" by holding
onto the hoop of the child in front of them. The "caboose" does not have a hoop, but simply
holds onto the child's hoop in front of her.
The conductor calls out, "All aboard," and the engineer starts the engine.
The engineer controls the train, making it go fast or slow.
Make sure the children take turns playing different roles.

Are there children in your classroom who
use a wheelchair? Include them in the train
by asking them to hold onto the hoop
of a child in front of them.
Ask others to take turns pushing the child's chair.

Hoop Play

Materials
Hula-hoops or loops of fabric

What can a child do with one of the hoops?
Challenge the children to find different ways of moving and holding a hoop.
For example, a child can hold the hoop around her waist and waltz around the room.
Ask the children to place the hoops on the floor.
Encourage them to pretend to be puppies or kittens curled up asleep inside their hoop.
When you give them a signal, the "puppies" and "kittens" get up, stretch, and then take a walk.
When you signal again, they return to their beds.

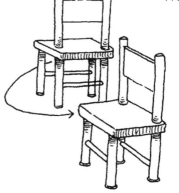

Hollow Block Play

Materials
Hollow blocks

Play "Going on a Bear Hunt."
Clap your hands against your legs
to the rhythm of a march chant and chant:

We are going on a bear hunt.
We are going to catch a big one.
Oh, no. We're not scared.

Then you come to a field of tall grass.
Scrape your hands together to simulate walking
through a field of tall grass and chant:

We can't go over it.
We can't go under it.
We can't go around it.
We have to go through it.

Continue on the bear hunt, going over a river, up and down a mountain,
through a swamp, through a dark forest, and any other places
until you come to a cave where there is a bear.
Then say, "Oh, no! A bear!" Go back through all the places until you reach home.
Then say, "We're not scared."

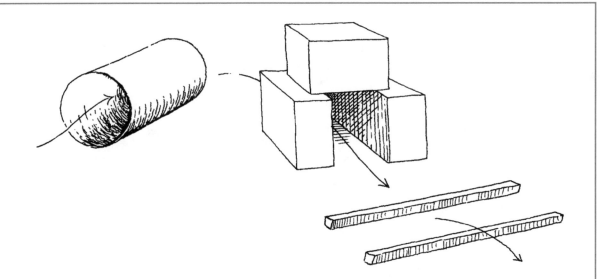

After the children have had fun going on a bear hunt, encourage them to build
their own bear hunt obstacle course using hollow blocks.
They can build an obstacle course of rivers, hills, mountains, or anything they want.
After they finish building, encourage them
to go on a bear hunt. Before they go on the hunt, safety proof their obstacle course,
making sure that the blocks are safe to go around or to actually climb on.

Connecting Home and School

Make the home-school connection
by taking photographs of the children building a bear hunt obstacle
course with blocks and then going on a bear hunt.
Duplicate and send home copies of the "Bear Hunt"
poem.

Thinking Children: Time to Study, Think, and Learn

Just as children are filled with energy, they are also filled with curiosity. They want to learn all about the world in which they live. Their drive to know and understand may be related to their need to achieve mastery over themselves and their world. In their drive to know, children use all the thinking processes of scientists. They observe, question, advance hypotheses, collect and analyze data, and reach conclusions. A rainy day gives you many opportunities to tap into children's natural curiosity and utilize all of their thinking skills as they observe and study rain.

Measure Rain

Materials
Plastic bucket or container
Ruler or other measuring device
Paper and pen

Explain to the children that scientists measure things. Start the practice of measuring rain.
Make a rain gauge by placing a clear plastic bucket or other container in an open spot to collect rain.
Help the children measure the rain that falls into the bucket.
Keep a record of how much rain falls on a given day. Graph the results.

Connecting Home and School

Make the home-school connection by sending home a note asking parents to help their children measure rain at home (see sample note on page 29).

Dear Families,

Have your children been telling you about their play with rain? One of the things we are learning as we play with rain is the concept of measurement. You may want to join us in measuring rain.

Place a clear plastic cup or container outside to collect rainwater. After it rains, measure the water in the container. There are a variety of ways you can measure it. You could pour it into a measuring cup and see how many cups of rain you collected, measure the depth of the rain in the container with a ruler or other measuring tool, or pour it into a glass to see if you've collected an entire glassful of rain.

Keep in mind that children at this age will only be interested in the **idea** of measuring something. However, this interest forms a foundation for them to understand that things can be measured and, later, for learning how to use standard measures.

Thank you for reinforcing your children's classwork at home.

Sincerely,

What Rain Does

Materials
Eyedroppers
Containers of water
Variety of materials (see activity)
Drawing paper and materials
Little Johnny Raindrop by James Chappell

Ask the children to stand by the windows and watch raindrops falling on the glass.
Ask them to observe what happens when a drop hits the glass. Does it move up or down the glass? Which drops go the fastest?
Experiment putting drops of water on different surfaces inside the room using eyedroppers.
Ask the children to find out what happens when they place a drop of water on:

★ plastic

★ wooden and plastic blocks

★ pieces of aluminum foil, waxed paper, and plastic wrap

★ doll clothes

★ construction paper

Tilt glass, wood, and other non-penetrable materials and observe what the drops do.
Ask the children to sketch how the raindrops react on different surfaces.
With the children, draw conclusions about how the drops hold
their shape and travel on different surfaces.
Where else can children find raindrops? If it is raining lightly,
you might go outside and see if the children can catch a raindrop
on their tongues or in their hands.
Older children could try to hold a raindrop in their hand.
Ask them to place a drop of water on one finger and gently bring their thumb up
to touch the drop. What happens if they slowly, slowly take their finger away?
After the rain has stopped, go outside to look for raindrops.
You might find raindrops collected on the grass, leaves, or play yard equipment.
Read *Little Johnny Raindrop* by James Chappell to the children. It is a story about a raindrop.
Encourage the children to write and illustrate their own stories about raindrops.

Rain Changes What You Wear

Materials

Clipboards, paper, and markers

Start by asking the children to think about how rain changes their day.
First of all, what clothing did they wear to school today? Why?
Take a classroom survey of what the children wore to school.
Older children can take their own surveys as well as a survey of the class down the hall. Give them a clipboard and paper to record their findings.
Following is an example of a recording sheet. Children will ask, "What clothing did you wear because of the rain?"
Then, they can check off the children's responses.

Rainy Day Clothes

	yes	no
Boots		
Raincoat		
Hat		
Umbrella		

Rainy Day Clothes Are Different

Materials

Variety of waterproof and non-waterproof clothing
Eyedroppers
Containers of water
Clipboards
Paper and markers

With the children, take a close look at waterproof clothing,
such as a raincoat, hat, or boots. What material is the coat made of?
Compare the piece of waterproof clothing with a non-waterproof piece of clothing.
How do they differ? (For example, the waterproof material is probably slick and shiny.)
Now experiment with rain.

Set up a table with a couple of eyedroppers and samples of clothing made from different fabrics
(for example, cotton socks, cotton T-shirts,
cotton underwear, woolen mittens, slick rain hats, rubber boots,
umbrellas, or just a piece of vinyl).
Explain to the children that they are going to be scientists, and just like scientists,
their goal is to find out answers to questions. They are going to find out
what happens when they drop water onto each item.
Encourage the children to use a clipboard and paper to record their findings.
After the children have played around awhile with the water and the materials,
gather them together to reach some conclusions. Ask them what happened
when they dropped water on the sock, mitten, and other non-waterproof clothing.
Encourage them to compare it to the waterproof clothing.

Connecting Home and School

Make the home-school connection
by asking the children to find out
what clothing their parents wear
on a rainy day and why.

Which One Dries Faster?

Materials
Clothesline
Binder clips
Damp clothing

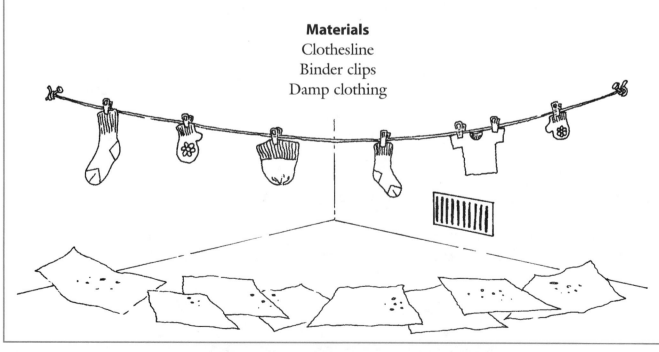

Hang a clothesline across the room or in one corner of the room.
Give the children a supply of binder clips and ask them to hang the damp clothing on the line.
Their goal is to see which pieces of clothing dry more quickly than others.
Ask them to describe their rainy day clothing, using words such as slick, slippery, or hard.

Rain Changes the Environment

Materials
Puddles by Jonathan London
Clipboards
Paper and markers

Read the book *Puddles* to the children. In this book, a brother and sister marvel
at the wonders of the changes that rain brings. They call puddles, "Big ones, little ones,
long ones, skinny ones—pieces of sky on the ground."
After you read the book, ask the children to observe
how the rain is affecting their own environment.
If there are not enough windows in your room for all of the children to look outside,
go to a place in the school where the whole group can observe
how rain changes the ground, sidewalks, buildings, flowers, and plants.
Ask the children to look for puddles and note where they are.
Are there puddles underneath plants or trees? On leaves?
Give the children clipboards, paper, and markers and
encourage them to draw or sketch the puddles.

What Are the Properties of Rain?

Materials
Pete's Puddles by Hannah Roche
Paper
Crayons, markers, or pens

Ask the children why they think rain collects in puddles
on the sidewalk, but not on the sand or ground.
If you are working with older children, you could ask them to relate their answers
to their experiments with waterproof clothing (see Rainy Day Clothes Are Different on page 31).

33

If the rain is light or has stopped, you might want to take the children outside
to splash, stomp, and slip around in the puddles.
When you go back into the classroom, three-year-olds might enjoy hearing you read *Pete's Puddles*
by Hannah Roche, which is the story of how rain changes a child's day.
Older children could use the book as a springboard to draw or
write their own stories of how rain changed their day.

How Does Rain Change Soil?

Materials
Rain-drenched soil
Containers
Box lids

Go outside with the children and collect a few containers of wet soil. You may be fortunate
enough to have different types of soil around the school, such as sand, loam, or clay.
Bring the soil back to the classroom and transfer it to box lids.
See how long it takes for the different soils to dry.
Does it take different types of soil longer to dry?

Connecting Home and School

Extend the activity by asking
parents to collect samples of soil
from around their home to bring
to class. With the children, observe how the soils are
the same or different.

Watercolors

Materials
Watercolor paints
Large paintbrushes
Sturdy, heavy paper
Buckets or cans of water
Newspaper or table cover
Mushroom in the Rain by Mirra Ginsburg, optional
Paper and crayons

Children enjoy using watercolor paints on rainy days (or any day!). Rinsing out large brushes,
working on large pieces of paper, and watching the light, fluid colors
of the paint are both interesting and calming to the children.
Place watercolor paint, large paintbrushes, heavy paper, and buckets or cans of water
on a covered table and encourage the children to paint. (The paint in children's
watercolor tins is usually of poor quality, so instead use squares of professional watercolors.)
Enjoy the children's pleasure as they simply explore a media that may be new to them.
You might want to suggest a rainy day theme for their subject matter.
If desired, read Mirra Ginsburg's *Mushroom in the Rain* to the children. It is a Russian folktale
about little creatures taking shelter in the rain. Then ask the children to paint
their own story of children, people, or animals hiding from the rain.
Another idea is to encourage them to use crayons to draw themselves walking in the rain.
Then, demonstrate how to make rain by washing over their drawings with gray watercolor paints.

Literate Children

What a great day for literature! After all, "Rain is falling on my window, on the trees tall and brown,

rain is falling in the garden, in the city and the town!"

April Rain Song

Materials

The Collected Poems by Langston Hughes

Paper

Markers or crayons

Read "April Rain Song" by Langston Hughes to the children. The poem begins,

"Let the rain kiss you.

Let the rain beat upon your head with silver liquid drops."

After you read the poem, read it again. This time pause before saying key words.

For example, say, "Let the rain kiss …." and wait for the children to fill in the missing word.

Next, ask them to say the poem with you.

You might want to copy the first two lines of the poem for the children to illustrate. Encourage

the children to draw their own idea of raindrops.

Finally, Rain!

Materials

Come On, Rain! by Karen Hesse

If you're experiencing a summer shower or a rain that breaks a long drought, read *Come On,*

Rain! by Karen Hesse to the children. It is a story about a sudden summer shower.

It is filled with poetry as well as hope and anticipation.

Are You Crying?

Materials

A Drop of Rain by Wong Herbert Yee

Read *A Drop of Rain* by Wong Herbert Yee to the children.
It is actually more of a story about babies than rain.
Preschoolers will delight in hearing about a family who thinks their baby
is crying because raindrops have fallen on its face.

A Rainy Day Poem

Materials

Paper and markers

Make up your own rainy day poem with the children. Begin with:

Rain, rain, go away,
Little children want to....

Ask the children to fill in the missing word or to continue the sentence.
Write each response on a chart and repeat until all the children have had a turn telling what little
children want to do on a rainy day.

Rain Song

Materials

Rain Song by Lezlie Evans
Paper and markers

Read Lezlie Evans poetic *Rain Song* to the children.
The story begins with the rumble of thunder, then describes leaves stirring and swirling,
and raindrops plip, plopping, drip, dropping, splitter, split, splatting everywhere!
Ask the children to think of other words to describe the rain.
List their words on a chart.

Rainy Day Books

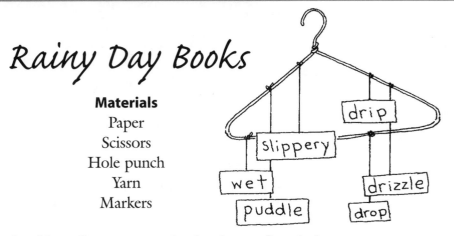

Materials
Paper
Scissors
Hole punch
Yarn
Markers

Make rainy day booklets. Cut out paper in the shape of a raindrop,
put a few pieces of paper together and punch holes through them.
Tie the pages together with yarn.
Give each child a booklet and encourage her to write her own rainy day story.
Encourage the children to draw or write about some of the experiences
they've had with rain, or they can make up their own raindrop story.
For the most part, children will use their own invented spelling as they write.
If desired, add a hanger full of rainy day words in the Writing Center.
Ask the children to "read" their stories to the others when they have finished.

Keep in mind that rainy day literature doesn't have to be about rain.
You might want to start a rainy day story hour tradition. Use a discarded beach or other umbrella
and hold a "Told Under the Green Umbrella" (or whatever color) story time.

Connecting Home and School

Make copies of the poems and list
the books you've read in class so
parents can say the poems with
their children and know what
books their children enjoy. Suggest that parents read
these books at home to their children.

A rainy day lends itself to reflecting, being still, and listening to your own thoughts
or to the soothing sounds of the falling rain.

Listening to the Rain

Materials
Listen to the Rain by John Archambault, James Endicott, and Bill Martin, Jr.

Begin by asking the children to listen to the rain. What does the rain sound like?
How does the rain make children feel?
Read *Listen to the Rain* to the children. It is the story about the sounds and silences of the rain.
Ask the children to listen to the rain again. Can they tap their fingers on a tabletop to mimic the
quiet, gentle sound of the rain? *Shh, shh, quiet, quiet.*
What words would they use to describe the rain? Would they use the same words as the author,
such as *slow, soft sprinkle, drip-drop tinkle, the sounding pounding rain?*

Collect My Thoughts

Materials
Blanket or sheet
Table, hollow blocks, or large box
Pillows, books, and netting
Mushroom in the Rain by Mirra Ginsburg

When young children are in groups for any length of time,
they will need to go off and be by themselves to calm down,
collect their thoughts, and just rest from the stresses of being with others.
On a rainy day, build a hiding place by:
★ covering a table with a blanket, leaving space for a door.
★ using a blanket to cover the top of a building of hollow blocks.
★ bringing out a large box (for example, a refrigerator box) for children to crawl in and be alone.
If they want, they can paint the outside of this hiding place.
★ arranging a quiet corner in the room with pillows and books.
Drape a piece of netting over it.

39

After the children have had some time to be by themselves, reread Mirra Ginsburg's *Mushroom in the Rain*. After you read the story, encourage the children to use any of their hiding places to act out being the ant, butterfly, bird, and other animals hiding in the rain under a mushroom.

Assessing and Evaluating

What Did the Children Learn?

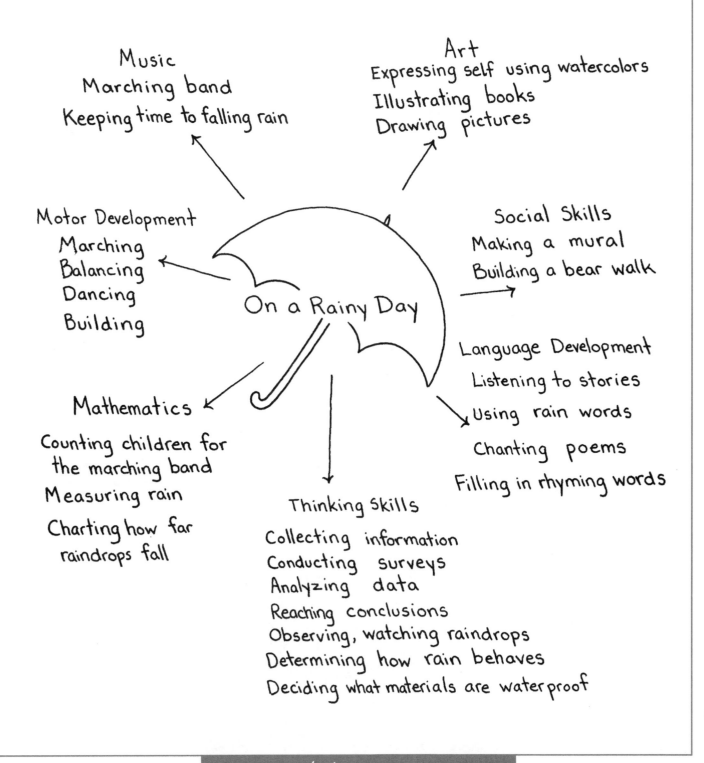

Music
Marching band
Keeping time to falling rain

Art
Expressing self using watercolors
Illustrating books
Drawing pictures

Motor Development
Marching
Balancing
Dancing
Building

Social Skills
Making a mural
Building a bear walk

On a Rainy Day

Language Development
Listening to stories
Using rain words
Chanting poems
Filling in rhyming words

Mathematics
Counting children for
the marching band
Measuring rain
Charting how far
raindrops fall

Thinking Skills
Collecting information
Conducting surveys
Analyzing data
Reaching conclusions
Observing, watching raindrops
Determining how rain behaves
Deciding what materials are waterproof

CHAPTER 2

Playing to Learn on a Hot and Sunny Day

On hot, sunny days, when you tell the children it's time to go outside and play, they may say, "No! It's too hot to go out!" Often, many days seem just too hot, humid, and hazy to go out and play. But there is still plenty of learning to do both indoors and outdoors on those days.

Of course, you have to plan ahead to make hot and sunny days not only enjoyable, but also safe. Establish some safety rules and procedures, starting with a sunscreen policy. Ask parents to provide children with sunscreen, hats, and bathing suits that they can keep at the center or preschool.

Find a cool, comfortable place and gather the children together to make plans for a hot and sunny day. Thinking ahead and anticipating events yet to come are sometimes the most enjoyable times of any event. And, when children engage their minds in deciding what to do, setting goals and finding ways to achieve them, and then carrying out their plans to completion, they are learning to think. Later, as the children reflect on the day's events, they will not only experience the joy of achievement, but will also gain the skills of remembering, recalling, and expressing the feelings, ideas, and emotions they've experienced.

Think of hot and humid days as opportunities for children to take part in planning their own learning experiences. This help creates truly enjoyable hot and sunny days filled with learning experiences that:
★ foster planning and reflection
★ introduce the physical sciences
★ provide a variety of language experiences

This chapter offers a variety of learning experiences and activities that will engage children's hands and minds. Read over the experiences and select those that fit your goals and the children's needs. Then, collect and organize the materials you will need to carry out the experience.

Planning and Reflecting Children

While you and the children are cool and comfortable inside, make "cool" plans for play and learning outdoors. Make plans for:
★ what the children will do and with whom
★ hydration and refreshments
★ shade

Making Plans

Materials

Chart paper

Markers

Tell the children that they are going to make plans for the day.

Sing:

What will we do? What will we do?

What will we do when we all go out to play?

Then ask the children what they would like to do and list their ideas on a chart.
When children offer suggestions, help them make plans to carry them out.
For example, say, "That's a good idea. I'll get the boxes, scissors, and tape,
and you can collect the papers you'll need. Who else wants to work with you?"
You may have to prompt younger children by saying something like,
"We'll take out the housekeeping equipment and have water to use for cooking,"
or "We could move the blocks outside on the sidewalk."
Or you might list other activities you have planned.

Books

Materials

Greetings, Sun by Phyllis Gershator, *Chloe's Sunny Day* by Annie Mitra,
or another book about a hot and sunny day

Books may stimulate children to think about what they can do on a hot and sunny day.
Read *Greetings, Sun* to the children. It is a story about a Caribbean boy and girl who joyfully
greet everything that catches their eye as they go through the day.
Children easily remember the chant,
"Greetings sun, greetings breeze, greetings toes and greetings knees."
Encourage the children to make up a greeting using their own rhymes
to celebrate beautiful things they see on a bright and sunny day.
Another good book to read is *Chloe's Sunny Day,* which is a simple story
about one sunny day in the life of a cat.
The story may motivate children to think about what they will do on their sunny day.

Reflection

Materials
Art materials or music, optional

At the end of the activity or day, ask the children to think about
and reflect on their experiences by:
★ Talking about them. Begin the discussion by asking the children to talk about the things they liked or disliked, what they would do differently the next time, or what they learned.
★ Organizing their experiences. Children in the British Infant Schools and the child care centers in the northern Italian town of Reggio Emilia organize their experiences by creating displays or constructing graphs with their teacher's help.
★ Expressing their experiences through drawings, paintings, stories, dance, or music.

Plan for Hydration

Materials
Coolers of water
Paper cups
Clipboard and paper
Crayons or markers

Just like marathon runners, construction workers, or any others who work outdoors in the heat, children need plenty of water or other fluids to drink when playing outside.
In addition to water fountains, take coolers of water and paper cups outdoors with you. Ask the children to plan:
★ Where on the playground they will place the jugs of water, cups, and a trash can.
★ How they will remember to stop for a drink of water during their play and learning activities.
Write the children's names on a piece of paper and attach it to a clipboard.
Ask the children to record the drinks they've taken
by putting a check mark next to their name each time they have a drink.
Later, determine how many cups of water each child drank during the day.

Our Own Drinks

Materials
Ingredients to make lemonade
Cups
Spoons

For variety, help the children make their own drinks.
With the children, plan how you will make the lemonade.
Gather the ingredients and mix them together.
Ask a volunteer to help with this activity because each child will make his own cup of lemonade.
Drink the lemonade.

47

Juicers

Materials

Three types of juicers (see suggestions below)
Picture directions chart (see illustration)
Lemons, 1 ½ for each child
Chart paper
Crayons, markers, or pens
Measuring cups and spoons
Sugar
Ice chips or cubes
Paper cups

Obtain three different types of juicers. It may take a bit of searching but try to find a hand juicer from
the 1930s or 40s (at a junk shop), a hand juicer from the 1950s or 60s, and an electric juicer.
Hang up a picture directions chart (see illustration).
When doing this activity, work with individual children.
Help each child thoroughly wash his hands.
Give each child three lemon halves to squeeze using both hand juicers and the electric juicer.
Ask the children which juicer they prefer to use and why. Record their answers on a chart.
Help each child use a measuring cup to find out which juicer
made the most juice and also record this on the chart.

Continue making the lemonade following the recipe chart (see illustration on page 47).
Label the children's cups of lemonade with their names and keep them
in the refrigerator until it is time to go outside.
Then, ask the children to bring their cups and decide where to drink their lemonade.
Make extra lemonade for helpers and aides.
Put the extra lemonade in a pitcher so everyone can have a second or third cup.

Summarize and Reflect

Materials

Paper

Crayons or markers

Lemonade Sun: And Other Summer Poems by Rebecca Kai Dotlich

That afternoon (or the next day), reflect on the experience of making lemonade.
Summarize the information on the charts and ask the children to explain how they made
lemonade, which juicer they preferred, and why.
Read the children the poem about making and selling lemonade from *Lemonade Sun: And Other
Summer Poems* by Rebecca Kai Dotlich.
Encourage the children to write, dictate, or draw their own story about
making and drinking lemonade in the shade on a hot and sunny day.

Frosty Chocolate Milk

Materials

For each child:

¾ cup skim milk

5 oz (140 g) paper cup

1 ½ teaspoons (4 g) instant chocolate mix

Spoon

Ice chips or cubes

On another hot and sunny day, make frosty chocolate milk.
The recipe per child is:
Pour ¾ cup skim milk into a 5 oz paper cup.
Add 1 ½ teaspoons of instant chocolate mix and mix it with the milk.
Stir. Add ice cubes as desired.
Reflect on the experience by asking the children to compare lemonade with the chocolate milk.
Ask them to decide which was the most refreshing, who liked the milk better
than lemonade, and what other flavors of milk they could make.
Take a vote to find out the class preference.

Connecting Home and School

Make copies of the recipes for lemonade and chocolate milk. Send home the recipes along with a note explaining how the children made them, what they said as they were making them, and how they enjoyed drinking their creations.

Make Yourself Some Shade

Materials
Varied (see suggestions below)

The following activities require both long-range and short-term planning. They will encourage the children to make plans, reflect on the past, and imagine the future.
The possibilities include:

★ Plant shade trees in the spring or fall. While the current group of children and teachers will not be able to enjoy shade from these trees, they will be able to enjoy watching them grow.

★ If you are working with four- and five-year-olds, help them create a time capsule for the children and teachers who will enjoy the shade in the coming years.
In the time capsule, place photos of the children shopping for and picking out the trees, digging the holes, and planting them. Ask the children to draw pictures and write stories of how and why they planted the trees and add these to the time capsule, too.

★ Plant a sunflower house. Plant sunflower seeds or seedlings in a rectangle shape.
Leave one side unseeded for the "door." As the sunflowers grow, prop them as necessary.
When they are fully grown, the flowers will bend down, forming a "sunflower house" filled with shade for children's play.

★ Plant a tent or two. Secure 3' to 5' (1 m to 1.5 m) dowels or bamboo poles in the ground in the shape of a teepee. Plant scarlet runner beans at the base of and in between each of the dowels. Because the seeds grow so quickly, even three-year-olds can record the number of days before the beans sprout, start climbing the poles, and cover the poles. You may have room in the play yard for several shady teepees in which children can play and hide.

★ Stretch a rope or clothesline across the play yard. Attach it to two trees or a corner of the fence and the building. Drape the line with sheets and discarded blankets for more shady places to play.

Artistic Children

About Hats

Materials
Hats, Hats, Hats by Ann Morris
Hats

Read *Hats, Hats, Hats* to the children. It is a book that portrays hats from around the world.
Encourage the children to brainstorm other types of hats.
Ask the children to bring in hats that their family members wear while working.
Or create a display of different hats from jockeys, firefighters, police officers,
cooks and chefs, hospital workers, and so on.
After the children have explored a variety of hats, ask them to think about
what kind of hat they need to keep the sun off their faces.
Make hats (see the following activity, Making Hats).

Making Hats

Materials
Chair
Wrapping paper, tissue paper, or newspaper
Masking tape

Designate a chair in the classroom as the "hat-making chair."
Ask each child to take a turn sitting in the chair.
Place one sheet of wrapping paper, tissue paper, or newspaper on the child's head. Using your
hands, press the paper around the child's head.

Then, take another piece of paper and place it crossways on top of the first piece and shape it to the child's head.
Continue adding paper until you have formed a firm "hat."
While the hat is still on the child's head, finish it by making a masking tape band.
Now the hat is ready to decorate (see the following activity, Decorating Hats).

Decorating Hats

Materials
Table
Tape, glue, hole punch, and fasteners
Decorating materials
Containers
Mirror

Place tape, hole punches, scissors, fasteners, glue, and a mirror on a table.
In individual containers, put different decorating materials, such as feathers, bits of material, paint, pieces of shiny papers, stickers, and anything else that would be useful for finishing a hat.
Place the containers on the table
Encourage the children to decorate their hats.
Explain to them that they can use the mirrors to check their work.

Shadows

Materials
Chalk or stick

Sunny days are good days to experiment with another type of shade—shadows.
Form teams and encourage the children to:
★ use chalk (on the blacktop) or a stick (in the dirt or sand) to draw around each other's shadows
★ try to step on each other's shadows
★ try a circus trick by standing on each other's shadow arms

Props and Shadows

Materials
Assorted props (see suggestions below)
My Shadow by Robert Louis Stevenson

Make shadows using props.
What kind of shadows can children make:
★ with an umbrella?
★ with boxes?
★ with wheels and other objects?
Take the children on a walk around the school and neighborhood
to find objects that make other shadows.
Discuss the shadows. Can the children identify what object makes the shadow?
Or do they have to look at the object?
Find the best and biggest shadow on the play yard and call this the "story shadow."
Gather the children on the story shadow and read them *My Shadow* by Robert Louis Stevenson.

Hand Shadows

Materials
Light source and nearby wall
Hand Shadows and More Hand Shadows: A Series of Novel and Amusing Figures Formed by the Hand
by Henry Bursill, optional

Is it too hot to make shadows outdoors? Show the children how to make
hand shadows indoors using a light source and a wall.
If desired, get ideas using Henry Bursill's *Hand Shadows and More Hand Shadows: A Series of Novel
and Amusing Figures Formed by the Hand* or another book on hand shadows.

Dissolving

Materials
Pitcher of water
Small, clear plastic cups
Wooden spoons and tray
Small plastic jars
Assortment of materials (see suggestions on page 56)
Clipboard and paper
Marker or pen

All the planning and creating the children have been doing leads them to question
and reflect on the nature of the things in their world.
As they do this, they are becoming acquainted with concepts from the
physical sciences including dissolving, melting, and the nature of water. For example:
★ What happened to the powered milk and sugar when the children made lemonade?
★ What does "dissolve" mean?
★ What happens when something dissolves?
★ Will they dissolve?
Set up an experiment so the children can learn more about how things dissolve.

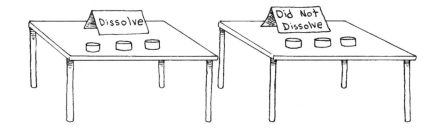

This activity can get messy, so it is good to do outside.
Set out a pitcher of water, small clear plastic cups, wooden spoons, and
a tray of small plastic jars half-filled with a variety of materials
(for example, sand, instant coffee, gravel, salt, sugar, and bits of paper or cloth).
Encourage the children to pour a small amount of water into a plastic cup, add a small spoonful
of any material, observe what happens, and record their observations.
Then, as a group, categorize the materials that dissolved and did not dissolve.

Melting

Materials
Block of ice or large, plastic milk or juice containers
Paper and markers, optional

Discuss the concept of melting with the children.
Ask them to reflect on some of the previous activities that involved melting. For example, what
happened to the ice when they added it to the lemonade?
If you can, obtain a block of ice for the play yard.
If ice blocks are not available, make your own large blocks of ice by freezing water
in large, plastic milk or juice containers.
Place a large chunk of ice in a sunny spot and another in a shady spot.
Encourage the children to play with the blocks. They can sit on them,
try to move them, put water or objects on them, and so on.
Listen to the children as they wonder about the ice. Add vocabulary words,
such as melt, heat, liquid, dissolve, and solid.
At the end of the day, discuss what has happened to the ice.
If they are interested, ask four- and five-year-olds to sketch the ice
at different points during the day.

What Else Melts?

Materials
Assorted materials (see suggestions below)
Cupcake tins
Clipboards and paper
Crayons or markers

Conduct an experiment to find out what else melts.

Gather a variety of materials, such as wax, crayons, chalk, bits of plastic, wood objects, playdough, clay, and so on. Place a different substance into each cup of a cupcake tin.

Group the children (four- and five-year-olds) into teams.

Give each team a clipboard with a piece of paper divided into two columns: MELT and DID NOT MELT.

Ask the children to place samples of the different materials in sunny and shady spots and record in pictorial or written form what melted and what didn't.

When everyone is done, ask the teams to report their findings to the group.

Water Words

Materials
Water source

What could be more appropriate on a hot day than water play? Not only is it a cooling, soothing experience, but also think of all the vocabulary children can learn when playing with water:

amount	funnel	strain
bubbles	heavy/light	stream
drop	pour	surface
float	quantity	volume
fluid	shallow/deep	waterfall
fountain	sink	weight
full/empty	slide	wet/dry
	slippery	

Water Math

Materials
Water

Buckets, eyedroppers, and other water equipment

Help the children count various things.

For example, they can count the number of drops of water in a dropper, the number of cups in a bucket, and the number of children who can work at a water table at one time.

Water Measuring

Materials
Water
Bucket or container
Measuring cups and spoons

Put out a bucket or container of water. Give the children measuring cups and spoons. Encourage them to use the cups and spoons to find out which bucket or container holds the most or least water.

Water Graphing

Materials
Paper, crayons, and markers

Make a graph of the children's findings and keep it as a record.

Cooperating

Materials
Water
Funnel
Piece of garden hose
Strainer
Containers

Encourage the children to work together using a funnel, piece of hose, and a strainer to fill containers with water.

Just Having Fun

Materials
Bubble mixture or liquid dishwashing soap
Water
Bubble-making tools, optional

Add bubble mixture or dishwashing soap to water to make bubbles.
Enjoy the children's laughter as they create bubbles with their hands or bubble-making tools, then watch the bubbles float away.

Water Play for Children With Special Needs

★ Arrange for a water table at wheelchair height.

★ Protect hearing aides from water, which could be damaged from water.

★ Cover electrical or other appliances on wheelchairs or other devices.

Basic Water Play

Materials
Swim suits and towels
Shallow wading pool or water table
An assortment of water play equipment (see suggestions below)

Water play requires a little advance preparation. Help the children change
into their bathing suits and have plenty of towels ready.
Basic water play involves filling a shallow wading pool or water table with water.
Add an assortment of water play equipment, such as empty plastic containers, pipes, egg beaters,
a strainer, sifter, plastic poultry basters, sponges, spoons, small shovels, and other things that are
safety-proofed and appropriate for the age and maturity of the children.
In addition to basic water play, there are numerous other water activities and experiences that will
keep the children engaged for hours. Some of these ideas are included below.

Plastic Squirt Bottles

Materials
Clean, plastic squirt bottles
Water
Empty six-pack holder
Chalk

Save a variety of plastic squirt bottles, such as ketchup, mustard, and detergent bottles.
Wash and sanitize them thoroughly.
Ask the children to help you fill the bottles with water. Place them in a six-pack holder with a
handle so the children can carry them around the play yard.
Encourage them to use the bottles to:
★ Squirt themselves when they get too hot or squirt at each other.
Ask the children who do not want to get squirted to tie a yellow ribbon
around the top of an arm to signal that they don't want to play.
★ Have a squirting contest. Using the same bottles, ask the children to stand
on a line and see who can squirt the water the furthest.
★ Hit a target. Use chalk to draw a circle with a bull's eye on the concrete or on the building.
Encourage the children to squirt and try to hit the target.
★ Create lovely designs with water on the sidewalk.
★ Make castles in the sand. The children can use the squirt bottles to keep
the sand moist enough to form castles, moats, forts, houses, and so on.

Sparkling Clean

Materials

Plastic tub

Hose

Plastic buckets

Sponges or washcloths

Squirt bottles of soap

Items to wash

Clothesline

Trikes or bikes

Fill a plastic tub with water.

Add plastic buckets, a hose, sponges or washcloths, squirt bottles of soap,

and things to wash, such as items from the Housekeeping and Dramatic Play areas.

Ask the children to begin by washing only one category of items, such as dishes or clothing.

The children can then wash the furniture, curtains, and so on, but it's best to begin with one set.

Find the best place to dry the wash. If desired, hang one clothesline

in the sun and another in the shade.

Encourage the children to observe where the clothes dry the fastest.

Or they can place items in the sun and shade to conduct the experiment.

Hold a trike or bike "car wash." Encourage the children to use a hose, buckets,

squirt soap, and some rags to clean the bikes and trikes.

If the children are interested, set up a business and wash the neighboring classroom's wheel toys.

Children can make pretend money to exchange and write up a list of rules and prices.

Help the children wash the ground floor windows of the building.

Wet and Dry Reflections

Materials

Wet and Dry by Jack Challoner

Ask the children to reflect on their water play experiences.

If you are working with two- and three-year olds, read the book *Wet and Dry* by Jack Challoner.

(This is a great book for this age group.)

After you read the book, ask the children to find things that are wet or dry in the play yard.

Paint the World

Materials
Small plastic or cardboard paint buckets
Inexpensive paintbrushes
Water

Are the children finished washing things? Then paint the world!
Pour water into small plastic or cardboard paint buckets and give the children inexpensive paintbrushes.
Encourage the children to paint the sidewalk and anything else they desire.

Go Fish

Materials
Tub of water
Plastic or wooden fish (or other objects)
Small fishnets, slotted spoons, and strainers
Set of plastic letters

Do you want to add some academics to all this sensori-motor learning? Play a "Go Fish" game.
Put plastic or wooden fish or other objects into a tub of water. Give the children small fishnets,
slotted spoons, and strainers to "catch" the fish.
First, play the game just catching fish and putting them back.
After the children have had plenty of fun catching fish,
take out the fish and put in some plastic letters.
Encourage the children to use the nets to catch the letters and say the letter name.

Mud Pies

Materials
Pile of dirt
Discarded pots, spoons, pie pans, and so on
Water
Buckets, watering cans, or hose
Small stones, sticks, leaves, or twigs
Paper and markers

61

Make mud pies. It's really, truly messy, but the kids are in their bathing suits and they can take one more run through the sprinkler before they dry off and come inside. All you need is:

★ A pile of dirt, or an area of the play yard in which children can dig

★ Discarded pots, pans, spoons, small bread, cake, pie pans, or other containers purchased from a local thrift shop or donated by families

★ Water in buckets, watering cans, or from a hose

Encourage the children to mix the dirt and water to make mud pies.

Show the children how to use small stones, sticks, leaves, or twigs to decorate their pies.

Ask the children to find out:

★ How much dirt does it takes to mix with water to make the "best" pie?

★ How long it takes a mud pie to dry in the sun?

★ How much does the same mud pie weigh when wet and dry?

If the children are interested, set up a "Mud Pie Bakery" so that others can shop for mud pies.
Help them make pretend money, decide on prices, and write lists and costs of cakes and pies for sale.
Continue the fun with language. Ask the children to write or dictate their "recipes" for special mud pies and make up a poem about making mud pies.

Children Experience Language

Too Hot to Move

Materials
Chart paper and marker or pen

Sometimes it is too hot to even move. On these days, find a quiet, protected, shady, or cool spot indoors or out and just sit, lay, or sprawl on the floor and be still.

Ask the children if they can be as still as still as can be. How quiet can they be?

A common phrase is: "As quiet as a mouse." Ask the children how many ways they can be quiet?
List their ideas on a chart.

Cool Poetry

Materials
Books of poetry (see suggestions below)

While the children are still and quiet, read them some beautiful poetry.
Ask a librarian to direct you to the books you need, or request the following books:
★ Jean Marzollo's *Sun Song*. The author uses lovely language
to describe the daily cycle of day and night.
★ Harry Belafonte's *Island in the Sun*. This is a song of tribute
to the beauty of Jamaica and our world.
★ Raffi has a book of songs to read to children. Get a copy of *One Light, One Sun* and read or
sing the stories about three families engaged in similar daily activities.
★ Nikki Giovanni's *The Sun Is So Quiet: Poems*. The lovely poetry collected in this book brings
children close to others in many cultures and settings.
★ Alma Flor Ada's *Gathering the Sun: An Alphabet in Spanish and English*.
The author uses the Spanish alphabet as the organizer of poems in
Spanish and English about those who work in the sun.

Tales About the Sun

Materials
Books of folk tales, myths, or stories about the sun

Are the children calm and quiet? It's time for some folk tales, myths, and storytelling.
Explain to the children that nearly every culture has tales about the sun.
Hot, sunny days are great times to acquaint children with one of these stories.
Explain to the children that the story is a myth (it's imaginary and not really true), but it was told
over and over and became a legend to the people who told it.
★ *Arrow to the Sun: A Pueblo Indian Tale* by Gerald McDermott is the story of the Indian rever-
ence for the source of life: the Solar Fire.
★ *The Day Sun Was Stolen* by Jamie Oliviero is based on the Haida Indian legend and tells of the
beginning of the world when Raven created all the animals.
★ *East O' the Sun and West O' the Moon: Fifty-Nine Norwegian Folk Tales* by Peter Christen
Asbjornsen is another book of folk tales about the origin of the sun.

What Did You Do on This Hot and Sunny Day?

Assessing and Evaluating

What Did the Children Learn?

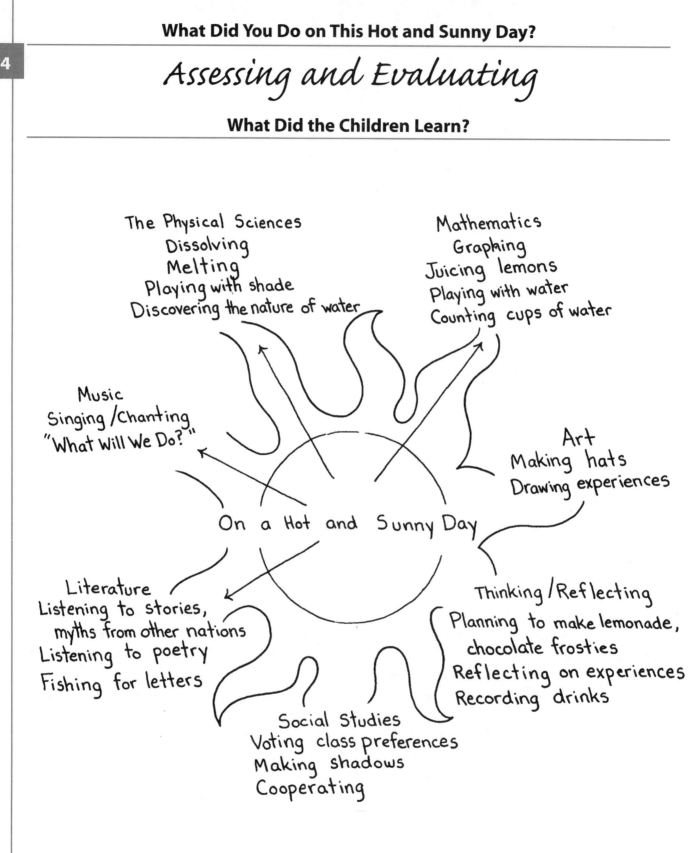

The Physical Sciences
Dissolving
Melting
Playing with shade
Discovering the nature of water

Mathematics
Graphing
Juicing lemons
Playing with water
Counting cups of water

Music
Singing /Chanting
"What Will We Do?"

Art
Making hats
Drawing experiences

On a Hot and Sunny Day

Literature
Listening to stories,
myths from other nations
Listening to poetry
Fishing for letters

Thinking /Reflecting
Planning to make lemonade,
chocolate frosties
Reflecting on experiences
Recording drinks

Social Studies
Voting class preferences
Making shadows
Cooperating

Playing to Learn on a Windy Day

"Who has seen the wind? Neither I nor you," wrote Christina Rossetti (1961),

and it is true! Neither you nor I have actually seen the wind,

and yet we know it is there. We feel and see the effects of the wind daily.

There are lots of things to do and learn on a windy day. Playing with and experiencing the effects of the wind may be children's first encounter with the concept that their earth is surrounded by atmosphere. As children observe and experiment with wind, they are forming beginning concepts of not only atmosphere, but also the force of the wind and its uses.

On a windy day children can:

★ *learn to observe the effects of the wind as it moves objects and things*

★ *chart the weather changes and force of the wind*

★ *try to catch the wind*

★ *observe the direction of wind*

★ *feel the force of the wind*

★ *listen to the wind*

This chapter offers you a variety of experiences with wind (too many for any one windy day). Pick and choose those experiences that seem closest to the children's interests, and those that would fulfill your program's goals.

Observing Children

The Effects of the Wind

Materials

Assorted materials, optional (see suggestions below)

Air is all around us! We live in it, we breathe it,
and we feel it as wind when it blows. But we can't see air.
Begin by making children aware of the characteristics of the atmosphere that surrounds our earth.
Then try some experiments with air. You might want to start by having the children become
aware of the air that they themselves can create.

To do this, try one of more of the following activities. Ask the children to:

★ feel their chests as they breathe in and out

★ listen to each other's breathing with a stethoscope

★ blow Ping-Pong balls across a table

★ make folded-paper fans to fan one another

★ keep feathers in the air by blowing on them

★ blow up water or other toys (Use new nozzles each time a child takes a turn.)

As the children do these things, encourage them to observe which way the balls, feathers, and other things move. Do the objects move toward or away from the children's breath?

The Wind

Materials
Poem about wind, perhaps from *January Rides the Wind* by Charlotte Otten

Read a poem about the wind to the children.

After you read the poem, take the children outside and look for the wind.

Ask them to look up in the sky. What do they see? They may see an airplane, birds, clouds, and perhaps a trail of smoke left by a jet plane.

Look around. What else do the children see that lets them know there is wind?

Do they see trees bending down; birds soaring on a wind stream;

or paper scraps, dust, and leaves blowing around the play yard?

Ask the children to determine which things in the sky and

on the ground seem to be moving the fastest? The slowest? At the same rate?

They might say that everything they see in the sky is moving at the same rate.

Ask the children to look again at the wind moving the leaves and other things on the ground.

Which of these is moving the fastest? Which flies the furthest?

Challenge their thinking by asking why they think this is so

and if there are ways they could find out.

Blowing Wind

Materials
The Wind Blew by Pat Hutchins
Paper, stapler, and crayons or markers

Read *The Wind Blew* by Pat Hutchins to the children.
It is a story about the wind that snatches things from children and blows them away.
After playing with wind (see The Effects of the Wind and The Wind on pages 66-67),
the children will be able to tell their own stories about how the wind
blew things away from them or how they "caught" wind.
Write a group story called "The Wind." Ask each child to contribute different ideas.
Or, encourage each child to keep her own "Wind Journal."
Make books by stapling together a couple of pieces of paper between
two sheets of construction paper. Title it "My Wind Journal"
and encourage the children to use it to record their experiences with the wind.

Wind Experiment

Materials
String or wire
Variety of paper (including cardboard and facial tissue)
Paper clips
Clipboards and paper
Markers

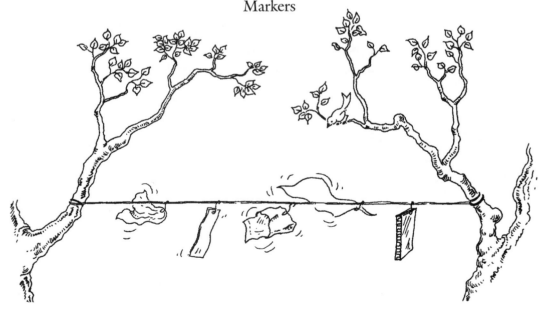

Stretch a string or wire lightly between two trees or other objects in the play yard.
Begin with a few pieces of different kinds of paper, cardboard,
construction paper, and a piece of facial tissue.
Open up a few paper clips. Attach a piece of paper to one hook of the opened-up paper clip and
hang the other end of the paper clip on the string.
Encourage the children to watch the wind blow the papers. Which blows the fastest and why?

Ask the children to find other objects to attach to paper clips, such as leaves,
different kinds of paper, small toys, or other objects.
Keep clipboards, paper, and markers handy so the children can sketch their observations.
Or, duplicate the following chart (see below) and encourage the children
to sketch the things that move the fastest or slowest in the wind.

Moves Fastest	Move Slowest

Find out how other things move in the wind. On different days, take feathers, a variety of papers,
streamers, and pompoms outside to find out how the wind affects them.

Clouds

Materials
The poem "Clouds" by Christina Rosetti
Camera and film
Chart paper
Markers

On another day, when the sky is filled with clouds, read Christina Rossetti's poem "Clouds,"
which begins, "White sheep, white sheep, on a blue hill."
Go outside with the children and watch the clouds go by.

Bring a camera to record the children's experiences with the clouds.
Ask the children to describe the clouds. What do they look like? How fast are they moving?
When you go back inside, recite the poem again. Ask the children to create their own poems.
Write their poems on chart paper and encourage them to illustrate them.
On another day, read the poems again and ask the children to recall
the day they went outside and watched the clouds.
If desired, duplicate the poems, scan in photographs of the children watching the clouds
and some of their artwork, and give the booklets to the children's families.

Clouds Are Different

Materials
The Cloud Book by Tomie de Paola

There are many different types of clouds. Read *The Cloud Book,*
which describes different types of clouds, to the children.
Go outside with the children and look up in the sky.
You might want to choose a day when the sky is filled with cumulus clouds.
These large clouds, which resemble cauliflower, are showy.
These are the clouds that take on different shapes and remind us of other things.

Clouds

Cumulus clouds are white, fluffy,
and shaped like cauliflower. These clouds
often signal the beginning of thunderstorms.
Cirrus clouds are high in the sky, thin, and wispy.
They sometimes look like tufts of hair. They are so
high and the air is so cold that the water they
contain is frozen into ice crystals.
Stratus clouds are flat, gray clouds.
Nimbus clouds are dark and threatening.

It Looked Like...

Materials
It Looked Like Spilt Milk by Charles G. Shaw
Sky blue paper
White paint
Paintbrushes
Marker
Stapler
Construction paper

Read *It Looked Like Spilt Milk* to the children.
Place sky blue paper, white paint, and paintbrushes on a table to make a book-making area.
Ask the children to make a "spilt milk" picture for a class book.
Encourage them to think of what the clouds looked like when they were outdoors,
and then paint a picture of a cloud that looks like something else.
Label each painting with the child's name and the sentence, "It looked like...,"
and add the name of the object that the child has painted.
Make a class book by stapling all the pictures between two pieces of construction paper.
Title the book, "Our Spilt Milk Book."
Read the book at Circle Time, and ask each child to tell a story about her painting.
Put the book in the Library Area so the children can enjoy reading it.

Predicting the Weather

Materials
Clipboard and paper
Markers

Five-year-olds can observe clouds to predict the weather.
Make a chart of the types of clouds (see following page) and then ask the children
to predict if it will rain or not.
Record whether their predictions were correct.

Charting the Weather

Day	Clouds	Will It Rain?		Did It Rain?	
		Yes	No	Yes	No

Catch the Wind with Parachutes

Materials

Lightweight cloth or piece of plastic bag
Scissors
Hole punch
String
Small weight
Paper and markers

There are many ways that people catch the wind and use its force.
Preschoolers are too young to understand how the wind produces electrical power,
but they can experiment with catching the wind and observing its effects.
Make a few parachutes to take outside. Cut out a 12" (30 cm) square
from lightweight cloth or a plastic bag.
Punch a small hole in the center and in each corner of the square.
Tie a string through each of the four corner holes of the cloth.
Tie all four strings together near their free ends.
Fasten a small weight (a metal washer works well)
to the free ends of the string.
Take the parachutes outside and
show the children how to fold the parachute
by holding the center and rolling
it toward the strings. Wrap the strings around
the cloth and toss the parachutes in the air
as high as they can go. After the children play with
the parachutes for a while, try some experiments:

★ Who can toss the parachute the highest?
★ How far do the parachutes fly?
★ How many times can the children jump on both feet before the parachute hits the ground?
Ask the children to look at the parachutes and describe how it looks
when it is first tossed in the air, when it fills with air, and when it falls to the ground.
Back in the classroom, encourage the children to draw themselves tossing parachutes in the air
(Seefeldt & Galper, 2001).

Observing Parachutes

Materials
Clipboards and paper
Markers

Give the children clipboards, paper, and markers and
ask them to record their observations of parachutes.
As they work, talk with the children and ask what they see and what they have chosen to draw.
Refocus their observations by asking them to look again
at the things in the sky and on the ground that are moving.

Reading About Wind

Materials
Gilberto and the Wind by Marie Hall Ets
Paper
Crayons and markers
Stapler
Construction paper

Read *Gilberto and the Wind* to the children, which is a story of a boy
who finds that the wind is a great playmate for sailing boats,
flying kites, and blowing other things.
Make a class book. Ask each child to contribute a drawing
of something they observed blowing in the wind.
Staple together all of their drawings between two pieces of construction paper.

Wind and Water

Materials

Sailboats, or materials to make boats
Wading pool
Water

A warm and windy day is great for sailing boats in a wading pool.
If you are working with five-year-olds, help them make their own sailboats.
Give younger children already-made sailboats.
Fill a wading pool with water and encourage the children to sail their boats.
Ask the children to observe the boats.
★ How do they move?
★ When are they still?
★ Can they make them move faster by blowing on the sail?
★ Can they position the boats to catch the wind?

Which Way Does the Wind Move?

Materials

Clipboards and paper
Markers
Windsocks, or materials to make them (see suggestions below)

Which way does the wind move? On different windy days, ask the children to observe things
moving in the wind and record the direction of the wind.
Purchase windsocks or make them using a loop of wire,
a weight, a piece of nylon stocking, and a string.
Hang the windsocks in several different places in the play yard
(for example, from the branch of a tree, on a fence, and on a post).
From time to time when the children are in the play yard,
draw their attention to the socks and recite the poem, "The Wind."
Ask the children if they can see the wind when they watch the socks.
Ask children (older than four) to watch how the socks catch the wind and change directions.
Explain that this tells them which way the wind is moving.
On other windy days, encourage the children to experiment
using different objects to find out the direction of the wind.

Catch the Wind with Kites

Materials
Kites, or materials to make them

Explain to the children that other things, such as kites,
catch the wind and allow them to see the wind direction.
Purchase paper kites (or make your own) for the children to fly.
You don't need one for each child, but make sure there are enough
so that each child gets a turn keeping a kite flying and bringing it down again.
Ask older children or volunteers to help the children get and keep their kite in the sky.

Making Kites

Materials
Catch the Wind! All About Kites by Gail Gibbons, optional
Materials to make kites, paper, and markers

Make kites with the children and invite a community group to come in and help
(for example, an older group of children, elder volunteers,
or a club such as a Boy or Girl Scout troop or Boys' and Girls' Club).
A good kite-making reference book is *Catch the Wind! All About Kites* by Gail Gibbons,
which is a guide to making the five basic types of kites.
Practice making kites with the volunteers beforehand and teach them how best to work with children.
This activity will involve children in:
★ writing an invitation asking the community groups to help them
★ reading the kite-making book and identifying shapes
★ planning for the volunteers' visit. How will they greet them?
Where will they put the volunteer's things? How will they decide whom to work with?
What refreshments will they serve?
★ interacting with others of differing ages
★ writing stories documenting their work
★ writing thank you notes

75

Reflecting on Wind and Kites

Materials
Curious George Flies a Kite by Margaret Rey

Do you have time to reflect on kite flying? Read *Curious George Flies a Kite* to the children. As usual, George's adventures will charm even the youngest children.

Kites in Different Cultures

Materials
Books (see suggestions below)
Paper and crayons, optional

For children who are four- or five-years-old, read stories about
the mythical nature attributed to kites in different cultures.
When reading these books, make the distinction between fact and fantasy.
Explain that these books are make-believe. The stories were created long ago
and are myths that are fun to tell, but are not true.
Four- or five-year-olds might enjoy:
★ *Kites: Magic Wishes That Fly Up to the Sky* by Demi. This is a Chinese story
about a long time ago when people sent kites up into the sky as wishes to the gods.
After reading the book, encourage the children to do some wishing.
If they could send a kite to the sky and get a wish, what would it be? If desired,
ask the children to draw the kite they would use and tell or write about their wish.
★ *The Emperor and the Kite* by Jane Yolen. This is the myth of an emperor's daughter
who spends her day making kites and one day rescues her father.

Paper Airplanes

Materials
Paper

Help older children make paper airplanes. To give them an idea of how to make paper planes,
show them the following basic design (see illustration).
Encourage the children to experiment and make all kinds and shapes of planes.
Take the planes outside and launch them in the wind.
Ask the children to observe which planes fly best
and identify their shape, size, and what they are made of.

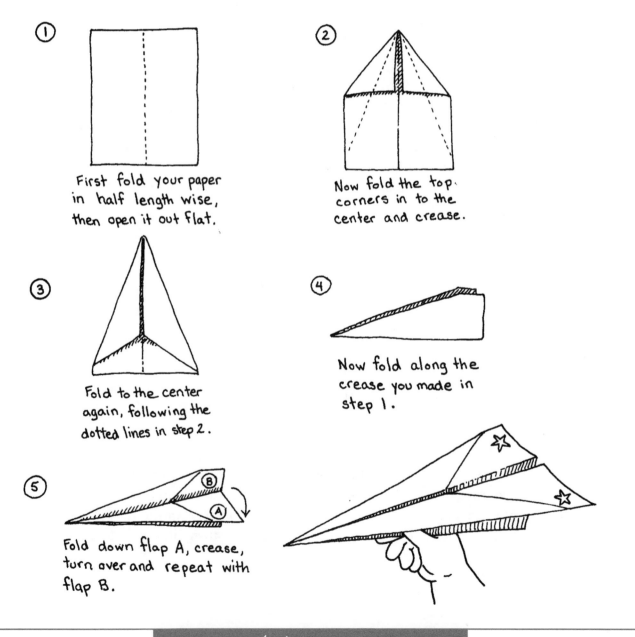

① First fold your paper in half length wise, then open it out flat.

② Now fold the top corners in to the center and crease.

③ Fold to the center again, following the dotted lines in step 2.

④ Now fold along the crease you made in step 1.

⑤ Fold down flap A, crease, turn over and repeat with flap B.

Just Seeds in the Wind

Materials
Milkweed pods or other seed casings

During the year, collect different seeds native to your area.
On a windy day, bring out milkweed pods for the children to play with.
Say the following poem:

Milkweed Seeds
In a milkweed cradle
Soft and warm.
Baby seeds are sleeping
Safe from harm.
Open up your cradle
Hold it high.
Come, Ms. Wind,
Help them fly.

Throw the seeds in the air and watch them fly. Ask the children to observe
how high they fly, where they fly, and which direction the wind blows them.
On another day, examine other seeds that are disseminated by the wind.
For example, maple seeds act like parachutes in the wind.

Wind Toys

Materials
Paper towel tubes
Paint
Paintbrushes
Tissue paper streamers
Paste, tape, or stapler

Make wind toys with the children. Save a bunch of empty paper towel tubes.
Encourage the children to paint them and decorate them as desired.
Paste, tape, or staple pre-cut long tissue paper streamers to one end of the tube. Encourage them
to take the toys outside and play with the streamers in the wind.

Wind Bag

Materials

Small zipper-closure plastic bag, large paper bag, or clear plastic bag

Encourage the children to "catch the wind" using small zipper-closure
plastic bags, large paper bags, or clear plastic bags.
Experiment with ways to catch and keep the most wind in the bags.

Catch the Wind with Bubbles

Materials

Bubble mixture
Bubble wands
Chart paper and marker

Bubbles are another way to catch the wind.
Encourage the children to try blowing bubbles with bubble hoops.
Ask them to watch as the liquid fills with air, and the bubbles blow away on the wind.
Back in the classroom, ask the children to describe the bubbles. What do bubbles do?
Make a chart titled "Bubbles" and ask the children to contribute words that describe bubbles,
such as *pop, burst, fly, go away, sparkle,* and so on.

Feel the Force of the Wind

Materials

None needed

Wind has a great deal of force.
Observe the force of the wind. On a windy day, take the children for a walk in the wind.
Walk with your backs to the wind. How does it feel?
Do the children feel a force pushing them along?
Now walk facing the wind. Do the children notice a difference? Which way is it easier to walk?
Ask the children to find a protected spot on the play yard where the wind doesn't hit them.
Encourage them to identify why they were protected.

Windstorms

Materials
Big Wind Coming! by Karen English, optional
Feel the Wind by Arthur Dorros, optional

At times, the force of the wind is responsible for a great deal of damage.
Children and their families may have experienced a windstorm in which trees broke,
houses were torn apart, and electrical wires were downed.
Or, they may have observed the force of the wind by watching televised pictures
of windstorms in other parts of the country or world.
With so many windstorms in the news, you may find it useful to read
Big Wind Coming! by Karen English, the story of how a rural African-American family
prepares for and survives a hurricane.
A softer story about the force of the wind is *Feel the Wind* by Arthur Dorros.
In this story, children are introduced to the ideas of why the wind
can gently rustle curtains or roar with the force of a hurricane.

Listening Children

The Sounds of the Wind

Materials
None needed

Ask the children to really listen to the sounds of the wind.
On a very windy day, go outside and listen to:
★ the sounds of the wind flapping the school, state, and our nation's flags
★ leaves brushing together as the wind whooshes through the trees
★ the sound of a piece of paper held up to the wind
★ a wind chime hung near your room

Do You Hear the Wind Singing?

Materials

Did You Hear the Wind Sing Your Name? by Sandra De Coteau

Watercolor paint

Paintbrushes

Paper

Read *Did You Hear the Wind Sing Your Name?* by Sandra De Coteau to the children.
This Oneida Indian tale puts children in touch with the changing seasons
as they are asked to use their senses to taste the first strawberries of the spring,
smell the cedar tree, feel the warmth of the sun,
and listen to the sound of the wind singing their name.
After you read the book, go outside (or listen to the wind from inside the classroom)
and see if children can hear their name sung in the wind.
Of course, they have to listen and pretend to hear a name, but it's fun to do.
Back in the classroom, encourage the children to paint the feel
and sound of the wind using watercolor paint, large brushes, and paper.

Describe the Wind

Materials

None needed

How would children describe the sound of the wind?
On other windy days, you might ask children to describe
how the sound of the wind makes them feel.
Ask the children to describe the sound of the wind when they:
★ listen to wind whistling around a building
★ hear wind chimes
★ listen to the wind rustling through the trees or tall grasses
Which sounds are happy, scary, sad, or funny?

Wind Instruments

Materials
An older child or volunteer who plays a wind instrument
Alligators and Music by Donald Elliott
Flutes by Barry Carson Turner

Invite an older child or other volunteer to come in and play a wind instrument for the children.
Ask the visitor if she can obtain a discarded flute or other woodwind instrument
for the children to examine before they come to the class.
Before the visitor arrives, read *Alligators and Music* to the children.
This entertaining story introduces children to a variety of musical instruments.
Or read *Flutes* by Barry Carson Turner, which is a small book
that introduces children to flutes around the world.
Ask the visitor to show the instrument to the children, name its parts,
and explain how wind (in this case the player's breath) is necessary to play the instrument.
After the performance, encourage the children to comment.
Ask the visitor to play a few more pieces.

Assessing and Evaluating

What Did the Children Learn?

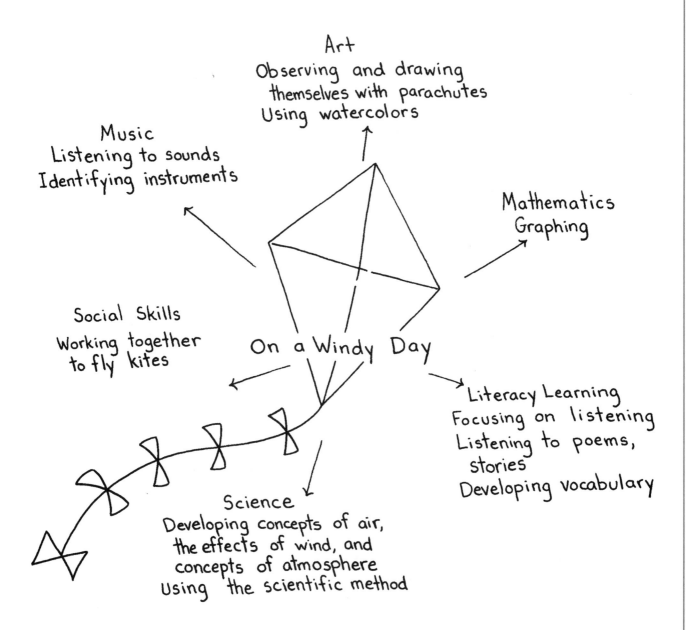

Art
Observing and drawing
themselves with parachutes
Using watercolors

Music
Listening to sounds
Identifying instruments

Mathematics
Graphing

Social Skills
Working together
to fly kites

On a Windy Day

Literacy Learning
Focusing on listening
Listening to poems,
stories
Developing vocabulary

Science
Developing concepts of air,
the effects of wind, and
concepts of atmosphere
Using the scientific method

CHAPTER 4

Playing to Learn on a Perfectly Beautiful Day

"Oh, what a beautiful morning, oh, what a beautiful day! I've got a beautiful feeling, everything's going my way!" As the song from Oklahoma says, there's nothing like a beautiful morning to make you believe that it's going to be a perfectly beautiful day. And it will!

It's a given that on a beautiful day, children will be able to take full advantage of the outdoors and engage in all types of play. Play is not a singular activity; rather there are many different types and kinds of valuable play that can take place on any day (and certainly on a perfectly beautiful day).

This chapter describes plenty of ideas for outdoor play on a beautiful day. Select ideas that match the developmental level and needs of the children you teach and the goals of your program. This chapter describes ideas for:

★ *exploratory play*

★ *constructive play*

★ *dramatic play*

★ *games with rules*

★ *play with language*

Types of Play

Exploratory Play

Infants, toddlers, and three-year-olds usually play by themselves as they explore their world and the things in it. They like to be with others, but they mostly engage in parallel play, sitting next to each other and even talking with each other, but each playing by themselves.

Constructive Play

Generally children move from exploratory play to constructive play as they mature. By the age of four, children begin to use objects to create something. For example, they stack blocks, roll clay into snakes, or name their scribbles.

Dramatic Play

Even though toddlers use objects to represent something else, such as feeding a baby doll with a block that represents a spoon or playing out themes with stuffed animals, trucks, and other toys, true dramatic play is the province of three- to five-year-olds. True dramatic play is complex and involves symbolic representation. For example, children may use a crayon to represent scissors. Children also take on the roles of others, pretending to be a mother, father, astronaut, or zookeeper.

Games With Rules

Three- and four-year-olds enjoy circle games that begin and end spontaneously.
Older fours and children who are five, though, are able to engage in group games with prescribed rules.
These games demand that children work together according to these prescribed rules.

Exploring Children

Much of toddlers' play is exploratory. Exploratory play means just that. Children do things
with objects to find out about the properties of materials, what they can do with them, and how to do it.
They may fill a cup with sand and spill it only to fill it again and spill it again.
Toddlers usually play by themselves while enjoying the company of others. But preschoolers and older children
also need time to play by themselves, explore their environment, and practice their skills and gain new ones.

As children grow and mature, the nature of their play changes. As toddlers grow and mature, they are more
intent on playing with others (although they still play by themselves in the company of others).
Unlike toddlers, who jump from one thing to another, preschoolers begin to focus their attention
on building, constructing, working puzzles, and making and carrying out plans.

Toddlers and Boxes

Materials
Empty cardboard boxes
Other objects, optional

A perfectly beautiful day can be filled with exploratory play.
Toddlers will enjoy practicing locomotor skills.
Bring the toddlers outdoors to a grassy section of the yard.
Take off their shoes so they can feel
the grass under their feet. Give the toddlers
a collection of empty cardboard boxes
to push around or fill with other cardboard
boxes, leaves, or other objects. Tip over a
couple of boxes on their sides and watch as toddlers
fill the boxes with themselves.

87

Toddlers and Cars

Materials
Trikes, old-fashioned "kiddie cars," and bikes without pedals

Provide old-fashioned "kiddie cars," trikes, and bikes without pedals
(so the toddlers can push them). Encourage the toddlers to ride or push them.

Toddlers and Dump and Fill

Materials
Assorted items (see suggestions below)
Funnels
Plastic boxes

A favorite activity of toddlers is to "fill and spill."
Give the toddlers assorted materials, such as large beads, seedpods, parquet blocks, acorns, and
other objects that are too large to be swallowed or stuffed into noses and ears.
Provide funnels and plastic boxes and encourage them to fill and spill.

Toddlers and Pull Toys

Materials
Empty oatmeal boxes
String

Toddlers like to pull toys.
Make your own simple pull toy.
String together a few empty oatmeal
or other boxes to make a train
for toddlers to pull.

Toddlers, Boxes, and Blocks

Materials
Boxes
Blocks or other objects
Tissue paper, optional

Put blocks or other objects into boxes.
Give the toddlers a couple of the filled boxes to play with.
If desired, fill the boxes with tissue paper. However, only do this if you can watch the children closely so they hold and crumple the paper, but do not eat it.

Toddlers and Dumping

Materials
Assortment of objects
Plastic dish, box, bowl, or bucket

Put an assortment of objects into a plastic dish, box, bowl, or bucket for toddlers to bang around or dump out and put back in again.

Toddlers and Tubes

Materials
Empty tissue box, paper towel or toilet paper tubes, plastic and wooden spools

Give the toddlers an empty tissue box, toilet and other paper rolls, and plastic and wooden spools.
Encourage them to sort, stack, and explore the materials.

Toddlers and Bracelets

Materials
Plastic adult bracelets

Toddlers will enjoy playing with a stack of plastic adult bracelets.

Toddlers and Sand

Materials
Fresh sand
Shovels

Children enjoy shoveling piles of sand.
When you have fresh sand delivered for the sandbox,
ask the deliverers to dump a pile of sand next to the box.
Give toddlers and preschoolers shovels and watch them get excited!
They may not actually get the sand in the box, but it's the joy of shoveling that counts.

Preschoolers and Tunnels

Materials
Empty grocery boxes

Preschoolers enjoy exploring on a perfectly beautiful day just as much as toddlers do.
Cut off the ends of empty grocery boxes.
Make a tunnel by lining up the boxes in a row.
Encourage the children to explore crawling through the tunnel.

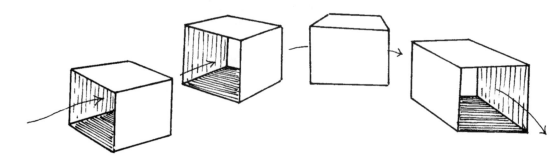

Preschoolers Finding Out How Things Work

Materials
Table
Tools, such as screwdrivers and pliers
Discarded small appliances, such as alarm clocks and phones

Taking things apart to see how they work is a joy-filled activity for preschoolers.
Place a table in the shade and put screwdrivers, pliers, and other tools, discarded alarm clocks, phones, and instrument panel boards on it.
Encourage the children to take the items apart.
Make sure to safety-proof all the objects. They must be free from sharp or small parts that could be swallowed, electrical parts, or glass and breakable parts.

Put It Together and Take It Apart

Materials
Large nuts and bolts
Pieces of PVC plumbing pipes
Broken toys and objects
Joining material
Building toys

Putting things together and taking them apart is a great discovery activity. You might want to ask a volunteer, perhaps an older child in the school, to help the children.
Give the children:
★ large nuts and bolts
★ plastic PVC plumber's pipes and pieces
★ broken toys, dolls, toy trucks, cars, or anything else that is broken,
and joining material for children to put the things back together again.
★ Tinker Toys or other building toys to put together

Preschoolers and Magnifiers

Materials

Magnifying glass, telescope, or materials to make a magnifying glass

Encourage the children to explore their world using a magnifying glass or telescope.
Show children under five how to use plastic magnifying glasses.
You can teach some five-year-olds how to use a telescope by closing one eye and looking through
the glass. Keep in mind that not all children will be able to achieve this skill.
Make a magnifying glass for younger children using a bucket and plastic wrap (see illustration).

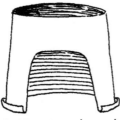

bottomless bucket
cut side out

stretch clear
plastic wrap
around, secure
tightly.

puddle of
water

look at insects
and leaves under
the bucket.

Exploring Sand

Materials

Sand and sandbox
Old kitchen items (see suggestions below)
Plastic squirt bottles
Water
Chart paper and marker
Scale

Go to a local thrift shop and buy a bunch of old household items,
or ask parents to donate items. Find:
★ baking pans
★ buckets
★ coffee pots
★ cookie cutters
★ egg beaters
★ funnels
★ measuring cups

★ muffin tins

★ pie tins

★ pitchers

★ plastic boxes or other containers with and without holes

★ plastic or metal salt shakers

★ shells

★ sieves

★ slotted spoons

★ spades

★ trowels

Safety-proof all of the items.
Add the items to the sand box, along with plastic squirt bottles filled with water
so the children can keep the sand wet enough to mold if they desire.
Chart the learning that takes place when children play with sand.
This activity helps the children develop vocabulary words, such as:

★ fill

★ fine

★ grain

★ gritty

★ heavy

★ light

★ modeling

★ molding

★ patting

★ pour

★ shaping

★ shoveling

★ sift

★ spill

★ wet

Children also learn mathematics in the sandbox.
Ask the children to count the number of cups of sand a bucket or pail will hold,
or the number of children who can work in the sand area at the same time.
Weigh the buckets, pails, or other containers of sand. Which contains the most sand?
Which one weighs the most? Which one weighs the least?
The sandbox is also a place to develop cooperative play skills.
Children learn how to cooperate so they can build castles or forts, or make pies to bake.
They also learn to cooperate when they keep the sand out of each other's faces and work spaces.

Constructive Children

Constructive play begins soon after infancy. For example, toddlers put blocks in a row and move a car over them, stack blocks to make a tower, or arrange them in a rectangular shape to make a house. By the age of three or four, children will begin to construct more complex objects that represent things and ideas. Children enjoy constructing by themselves, in the company of others, and as they grow and mature, with others.

Boards and Wooden Boxes

Materials
Boards and wooden boxes
Blocks

Both toddlers and preschoolers will find many uses for boards and wooden boxes.
Ask parents or community volunteers to help you construct planks with cleats
and wooden boxes with and without slats. (The cleats on the boards permit safe hooking
onto a box or another board.)
Because the boards and boxes are too heavy for a child to move by himself,
this type of construction demands language, communication, and teamwork skills.
Constructive play involves work with smaller objects as well.
Bring an assortment of blocks outdoors for children to build on a solid surface.

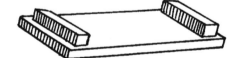

attach cleats or
blocks of wood

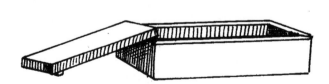

Building Structures

Materials
Empty cardboard boxes
Tape or other joining tools
Paint and paintbrushes
Buckets
Old sheets and blankets
The Big Brown Box by Marisabina Russo, optional

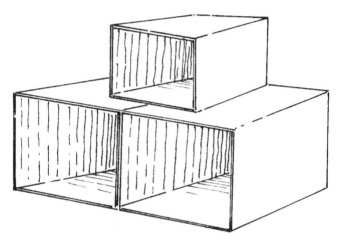

Give the children a bunch of empty cardboard boxes, tape, joining tools, buckets of paint, and paintbrushes and encourage them to construct a house, fort, boat, or whatever they want. Encourage them to arrange the boxes any way they want.
When the children start making houses, forts, or places to hide, give them:
★ small buckets of water-soluble paint and brushes to paint the boxes
★ discarded sheets and blankets to make roofs for the houses
★ additional equipment they may need to complete their house, truck, or fort
For example, if the children make trucks, you could bring in a discarded steering wheel and help them place it on a block inside the "truck."
If desired, read *The Big Brown Box* by Marisabina Russo before or after the children have built their structures.

Boxes by Delivery
Call your local appliance or household store
and ask if they would help equip your play yard
by dropping off empty cardboard boxes
on their way to or from a delivery.

Junk and Boxes

Materials
Box
An assortment of "junk" (see suggestions below)
Tool kit, such as glue, hole punch, duct tape, string, or pliers

Make a junk box to take outside by putting an assortment of junk into a box.
Continually collect junk for the box.
Practically anything can be junk, such as the plastic that separates cookies in a package,
Styrofoam peanuts or bubble wrapping from packages, all sizes of empty boxes, cupcake holders,
bits of ribbon, string, artificial flowers, shiny papers, paper plates, bags, feathers, and fabric scraps.
The children do not need any directions. All that is needed is lots of junk that seems to say
to the children, "Use your imagination! What and how could you use me to make something?"
Along with the junk box, provide a tool kit equipped with
different types of glue, a hole punch, an assortment of joiners, lots of tape
(including duct tape and clear plastic tape), string, and pliers.

Outside Clay

Materials
Clay
Covered bucket or plastic container
Pressed wood and plastic tablecloth, or picnic table

Make fist-sized pieces of clay and place them in a covered bucket
or other covered plastic container.
Give the children the clay and encourage them to explore.
Make a clay-exploring area by covering pieces of pressed wood with a discarded plastic tablecloth,
or use a wooden picnic table.

Outside Fingerpaint

Materials
Fingerpaint
Squirt bottles
Shiny paper
Table
Bucket of soapy water, paper towels, and trashcan

Fingerpaint outdoors.
Fill squirt bottles with fingerpaint.
Place rolls of shiny paper (such as shelf paper) and a bunch of squirt bottles
filled with different color fingerpaints on an outside table.
Place a bucket of soapy water, paper towels, and a trashcan next to the table for hand washing.

Outside Painting

Materials
Squirt bottles
Water
Chalk
Paint and brushes
Cardboard six-pack containers (from soda)
Brown wrapping paper

Ask the children to "paint" the sidewalk.
Fill squirt bottles with water.
Encourage the children to squirt a water design on the sidewalk, then "paint" over it with chalk.
Give the children "six-packs" of paint and brushes, along with a large piece of brown wrapping
paper. Encourage them to take these materials to a quiet spot and paint.
Or, attach large sheets of brown mural paper to a fence
and put the six-packs of paint next to them.
Add a bit of liquid detergent to regular paint, and if you have low windows or sliding glass doors
(and you're really brave!), ask the children to paint murals on the outside of the windows.
The soap will make the paint stick to the window and make it easier to remove after the next rain.

Dramatic and Cooperative Children

Socio-dramatic play and preschoolers are naturals together. Outdoors is a wonderful place for children to extend their dramatic play. There are a number of different types of props you can use to stimulate outdoor dramatic play.

Wheel Toys

Materials
Assortment of props (see suggestions below)

If you have wheeled toys, give the children some of the following props:
★ a tank vacuum sweeper to use as a gas tank so they can play garage and fill "cars" with gas
★ receipt books, pencils, and "credit cards" (plastic keys from hotels work great)
so they can pay for their gas
★ travel maps, tickets, suitcases, and backpacks so they can take trips in their cars
★ a variety of tools (safety-proofed), some pieces of hose, and flashlights for fixing broken vehicles

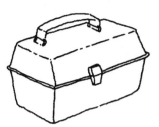

Work Props

Materials
Assortment of props (see suggestions below)

If the children see their parents go off to work and have visited them there, encourage their dramatic play by providing some of the following props:

★ work hats of all types, such as electrician, cowboy, firefighter, carpenter, painter, letter carrier, and construction

★ a few pairs of big, old work boots

★ lunch boxes

★ tool kits

★ briefcases

★ receipt books

★ purses and wallets complete with "credit cards," pretend money, receipts, and tickets

★ cell phones

★ any other tool or equipment representing the work that families do

Field Trip to Stimulate Dramatic Play

Materials
Assortment of props (see suggestions below)

If the class has visited a fire station, hardware store, plant nursery, bakery, or any other place of business or interest in the community, place related props outdoors for the children to re-enact their trip.
If you and the children have visited:

★ a fire station, put out a couple of pieces of hose, large boots, fire hats, and pieces of slick, yellow material that children can use to drape around themselves to represent firefighters' clothing.

★ a plant nursery, put out plastic flats, seeds for planting, boxes set up as a check-out counter, receipt books, play money, pictures of plants, seed and plant catalogs, and empty seed packets.

★ a shoe store, give the children hollow blocks and a bunch of empty shoeboxes. (They can use the blocks to set up a counter to pay for purchases and to make shelves to display the shoes.)

Housekeeping Play

Materials
Assortment of props (see suggestions below)

Stimulate outdoor housekeeping play by providing the following:
★ wooden crates, large hollow blocks, or other wooden boxes to serve as furniture
★ metal or plastic pots, pans, and dishes
★ a tool box for house repairs
★ a hose to water the yard
★ discarded cameras to take family portraits
★ discarded cell phones for communicating with others
★ dress-up clothes, old lace curtains (to use for dress up
or for playing kings and queens), pieces of velvet for capes
or other fancy clothing, hats, and ties

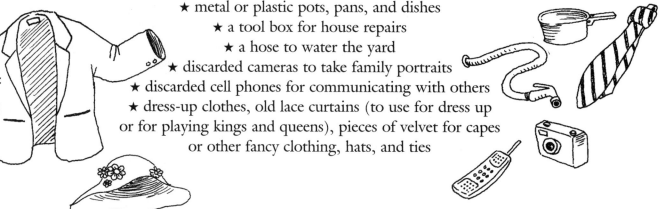

Children Play Games With Rules

Games with rules require a lot of sophistication to master. Children must be able to understand the group

organization required to play the game, remember the rules, take turns,

and give up some of their egocentricity to keep the game going.

Circle Games for Children Under Three

Materials
None needed

Children under the age of three are not terribly interested in or capable of playing organized
games. But some simple circle or singing games can be fun for young three-year-olds.
These simple games begin and end spontaneously as you take the hands of two or three children,
form a circle, and begin singing and walking in a circle.
Begin the game by singing one of the following songs while walking in a circle.
Children can drop out and others may join in as you sing:

Ring Around the Rosie
Ring around the rosie
Pocket full of posies
Tisha, tisha,
We all fall down.

Skip to My Lou

Skip, skip
Skip to my Lou!
Skip, skip,
Skip to my Lou!
Skip, skip
Skip to my Lou!
Skip to my Lou my darling!

Toodala

Everybody move too da la, too da la
Everybody move around too da la, la la dy.
Make some motions, toodala, toodala, toodala.
Make some motions, toodala, la – dala.

Running

Running up and running down
We're running up and running down.
We're running all around. (Or try hopping, skipping, jumping, or gliding.)

Skill Games for Children Under Three

Materials

Ball
Beanbags and empty boxes

Try one of the following games:
★ Sit on the floor with one or two toddlers. Spread your legs and
ask them to spread theirs, too. Roll a ball from one to the other,
encouraging them to try to catch the rolling ball between their open legs.
★ Stand close to one toddler and bounce a ball to him.
Try to bounce the ball near him so he can catch it on the way up.
★ Show toddlers how to toss beanbags into an empty box or container.

Circle Games for Threes and Young Fours

Materials
None needed

Three- and four-year-olds still will not have the skills and maturity required for playing group games with rules, but they can take part in simple games that begin and end spontaneously. Choose games that have no specific rules and do not require children to stand around waiting for a turn. Expect three- and four-year-olds to wander off to more interesting activities during the game and others who are not playing to join in for a few minutes. Try playing some of the following games:

★ Frog in the Middle—Form a circle and ask everybody to hold hands. Ask one of the children to be the "frog in the middle." Begin by walking in a circle while singing Frog in the Middle. As you sing, the "frog" tries to leave the circle and the children raise and lower their arms to prevent him from leaving. When the frog finally gets out, he chooses another child to be the frog.

Frog in the Middle
Frog in the middle and she can't get out,
She can't get out, she can't get out.
Frog in the middle and she can't get out,
Watch her hop and jump about.

★ Did You Ever See a Lassie—Ask the children to form a circle. Choose one person to be the laddie or lassie (tell them that laddie means boy and lassie means girl). The laddie or lassie will demonstrate a movement and the other children copy it. Then, choose a new leader. As a variation, use children's names instead of Lassie or Laddie.

Did You Ever See a Lassie?
Did you ever see a lassie, a lassie, a lassie?
Did you ever see a lassie go this way or that?
Go this way and that way and this way and that way?
Did you ever see a lassie go this way or that?

★ Punchenello—Ask one child to be Punchenello. This child will demonstrate a movement to the other children and they copy it. Then, choose a new Punchenello.

Punchenello
Oh, what can you do Punchenello funny fellow?
Oh, what can you do Punchenello funny you?
Oh, we can do it too, Punchenello funny fellow,
Oh, we can do it too, Punchenello funny you!

★ Charlie Over the Water—Ask the children to form a circle. Choose a child to be "Charlie" or "Charlotte" and ask him or her to stand in the center of the circle. Sing or chant the following song as you and the children dance around the circle with clasped hands.

Charlie Over the Water

Charlie over the water.
Charlie over the sea.
Charlie catch a blackbird,
But can't catch me.

At the word "me," everybody stops. If the child in the center can catch someone before he stops, that child becomes the next Charlie or Charlotte.
As a variation, use the children's names in place of Charlie or Charlotte.

Circle Games for Older Fours and Fives

Materials
See suggestions below

Try playing one of the following games:
★ Drop the Handkerchief—Ask the players to form a circle. Choose one child to be "It" and give him a handkerchief. "It" walks around the outside of the circle while everyone sings:

A tisket, a tasket
A green and yellow basket,
I sent a letter to my love,
And on the way I lost it.
I lost it. I lost it.

As the children sing, "It" drops a handkerchief behind one of the children, and then runs around the circle. When the child discovers the handkerchief behind him, he grabs it and tries to catch "It" before "It" reaches the empty place. The chaser then becomes "It."

★ Looby Loo—Ask the players to form a circle and walk around. While walking in a circle, sing Looby Loo and follow the motions. During the chorus, the children join hands and go around and around. During each verse, they stop and do the appropriate motion.
The verses are as follows: right hand, left hand, right foot, left foot,
my round head, my whole self.

Looby Loo
Chorus:
Here we dance Looby Loo.
Here we dance Looby Light.
Here we dance Looby Loo,
All on a Saturday night.

First verse:
You put your right hand in.
You take your right hand out.
You give your hand a shake, shake, shake,
And turn yourself about.

(Chorus)

Sing additional verses, substituting left hand, right foot, left foot,
my round head, and my whole self.

★ Round and Round the Village—Ask the children to stand in a circle and join hands. Choose one or more children to walk around the group while singing or chanting:

Round and Round the Village
Go round and round the village,
Go round and round the village,
Go round and round the village,
As we have done before.

At the next verse, the children inside the circle raise their arms and the children outside the circle walk around, going in and under the children's arms as everyone sings:

Go in and out the window,
Go in and out the window,
Go in and out the window,
As we have done before.

On the last verse, those walking around the circle choose other children
to take their place by standing in front of another child.

Now stand before your partner,
Now stand before your partner,
Now stand before your partner,
As we have done before.

★ Duck, Duck Goose—Ask all the players but one to stoop or sit in a circle. The one player standing is "It." "It" walks around the outside of the circle, touching each child lightly on the head and repeating the word "duck." This continues until "It" touches a head and says, "Goose."

The child called "goose" jumps up from the circle and chases "It." If the chaser succeeds in catching "It" before "It" reaches the vacant space in the circle, he becomes the next "It." If the player fails to tag "It," he returns to the space in the circle and the game begins again.

Chasing Games for Older Fours and Fives

Materials
None needed

Chasing games are as old as recorded history. Try some of the following:
★ Tag—Choose a child to be "It." "It" must chase the other children until he tags someone. This child becomes the next "It." Vary the game by playing:
    ★ Stoop Tag—The children being chased are safe if they stoop down.
    ★ Shadow Tag—Instead of tagging another child, "It" steps on the child's shadow to make him the new "It."
★ Wolf—Mark off a safety zone. Choose one child to be the wolf. The other children form a circle around the wolf and call out, "Wolf, wolf, are you ready?" The child replies, "No, not just yet, I have to put on my sweater," pantomiming the action. The children in the circle ask again, "Are you ready?" Each time they ask, the wolf invents a delay. Finally, the wolf takes the children by surprise and shouts, "I am ready! Here I come!" Then the wolf tries to tag another child before the child reaches the safety zone. The child who is caught becomes the new wolf.

Games of Skill for Older Fours and Fives

Materials
See suggestions below

Try one of the following games with the children:
★ Hide and Seek—Pick one child to be "It." "It" covers his eyes and counts to three while the others run and hide. "It" then goes off to find the others. The one he finds first becomes the next "It."
★ Basketball—You will need a small ball and a large basket for this game. Sit in a circle with the children and roll the ball to a child. The child stands and tosses it into the basket. (Children are free to move close to the basket.) When the child gets the ball into the basket, he chooses another child to take a turn.

★ **Tower of Blocks**—Make a tower of blocks.
The children sit in a circle around the blocks and take turns trying to knock the tower down.
When a child knocks over the tower of blocks, he picks someone to rebuild it.
★ **Toss Ball**—Stand in a circle with the children. Call the name of a child ("It")
and throw the ball into the air. "It" hurries and tries to catch the ball.
The child then calls the name of another child and tosses the ball in the air.
★ **Roll the Ball**—The children sit in a circle. One child rolls a large ball across the circle.
When the ball touches a child, that child picks it up and sends it rolling in another direction.
★ **Jump the Brook**—Draw two lines on the ground using chalk or making lines in the sand.
Begin the game with the two lines fairly close together. The children follow a leader and jump
over the "brook." When all the children have jumped, spread the lines a little further apart.
Repeat until the brook is too wide to cross. To add to the tension, each time you redraw the
brook, add a huge shark, an octopus, a stinging eel, or a large-mouth bass to it.

beginning

wider brook

Funny, Silly Poems and Stories

Materials
Suggested books include:
Beast Feast: Poems by Douglas Florian
Higgle Wiggle: Happy Rhymes: Poems by Eve Merriam
Let's Join In by Shirley Hughes
Finger Plays for Nursery and Kindergarten by Emilie Poulsson

End the beautiful day by playing with language.
Collect anthologies of children's poetry, rhymes, and jingles.
Some of the following books are full of funny, even silly, rhymes for children to play with:
★ Douglas Florian has collected humorous poems about animals in *Beast Feast: Poems*.
★ Eve Merriam has collected 25 tickle, wiggle rhymes for young children in
Higgle Wiggle: Happy Rhymes: Poems. The sound, feel, and action of the words
will appeal to all children, especially the youngest.
★ *Let's Join In* by Shirley Hughes is a collection of fun poems
and songs that will delight young children.
★ Emilie Poulsson's *Finger Plays for Nursery and Kindergarten* is one of the original fingerplay
books created for the first kindergarten programs in St. Louis, Missouri. It includes traditional
rhymes, such as "Here Is the Beehive," "Here's a Ball for Baby," and "Hen and Chicks."

What Did You Do on This Perfectly Beautiful Day of Play?

Assessing and Evaluating

What Did the Children Learn?

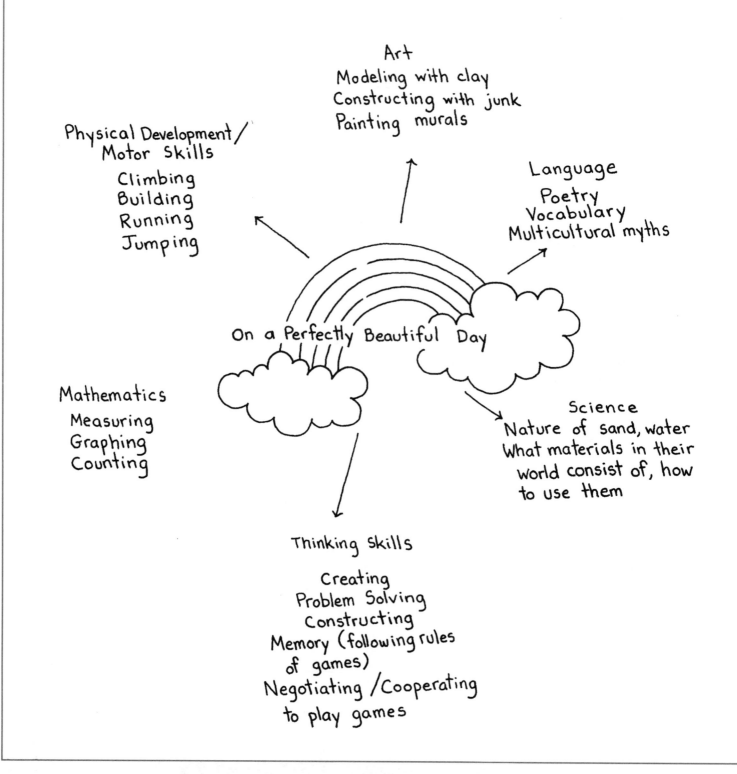

Art
Modeling with clay
Constructing with junk
Painting murals

Physical Development/
Motor Skills
Climbing
Building
Running
Jumping

Language
Poetry
Vocabulary
Multicultural myths

On a Perfectly Beautiful Day

Mathematics
Measuring
Graphing
Counting

Science
Nature of sand, water
What materials in their
world consist of, how
to use them

Thinking Skills
Creating
Problem Solving
Constructing
Memory (following rules
of games)
Negotiating/Cooperating
to play games

CHAPTER 5

Playing to Learn When You Have to Wait

HELPER CHART
Monday – Anton
Tuesday – Kimberly
Wednesday – Marc
Thursday – Shayla
Friday – Tony

Research shows that more discipline problems arise during transitions when children have to wait than at any other time during the preschool day. Of course, teachers of young children do not need researchers to tell them children get into trouble when they have to wait. Anyone who has worked with young children knows the problems that arise during transition times when children are asked to wait with nothing to do.

Good teachers solve a lot of the problems that arise during a waiting time by understanding that children need time to make a transition, planning ahead, and involving children in the planning.

Involving Children

When children are involved in setting procedures and routines, they are more likely to be able to accept waiting. For example, when you and the children set routines for washing before lunch or getting ready for or waking from nap, a lot of problems are avoided.

Giving Time

When children are given time to adjust to transitions, they are also more likely to adjust to changes and waiting. Giving the children a signal such as, "In about three minutes, it will be time to clean up," or "Take a few moments to finish what you are doing, then we have to get ready for the visitor," helps children prepare mentally and emotionally for transitions and waiting.

Even so, when children are asked to wait without having something to do, to think about, or enjoy, problems will arise. This chapter offers teachers appropriate activities that engage children's hands and minds when they have to wait. Some of the activities will last a moment or two of wait time, while others will last for many more minutes of unexpected wait time. Some of the activities give children the opportunity to practice developing skills, and others to use skills and knowledge they've already mastered. The skills can stem from any discipline area including:

★ language arts

★ mathematics

★ music and song

Literate Children

When you and the children have to wait, what better time to have a "poem in your pocket and a song in your head" (Martin, 1969)? When children have a song that sings to them and a poem that brings them happy thoughts, they won't even notice they're waiting for others to clean up, brush their teeth, or get ready to nap.

Poetry Bag

Materials
Fancy or decorated bag
Book of poems by Langston Hughes
Piece of plaid cloth

Turn a fancy velvet or decorated bag into a "Poetry Bag." In this bag,
place a book of poems by Langston Hughes and a piece of plaid cloth.
Show the children the piece of plaid cloth and ask them to describe it.
They may point out the colors and stripes.
Tell them that the name of this kind of cloth is "plaid."
Then, read the poem that begins, "The clouds weave a shawl of down plaid."
After you read the poem several times, play "My Turn, Your Turn."
Recite a line, stop, and then each child takes a turn reciting the next line.
This will help give the children ownership of the poem,
enabling them to recall the poem from memory.

ABC Bag

Materials
Plastic or wooden ABC letters
Fancy or decorated bag (see previous activity Poetry Bag)
An Edward Lear Alphabet by Edward Lear
Chart paper and marker

Start by putting the letters A, B, and C into the bag.
Ask a child to pick a letter from the bag and say the name of the letter.
Continue until all three letters have been removed.
Then read Edward Lear's *An Edward Lear Alphabet,* which begins:

A
A was once an apple pie…

B
B was once a little bear…

Continue by putting some of the other letters, a few at a time, into the bag.
(Don't put all the letters in at the same time.)

111

Encourage the children to make up their own rhymes about the letters.
Write their rhymes on a chart and title it "Our Nonsense Alphabet."
During another wait time, re-read the beginning verse and a little bit more.
Encourage the children to add more verses to the class "Nonsense Alphabet."
Recite the rhyme "A B C."

Great A, little a
Bouncing B!
The cat's in the cupboard
And can't see me!

Continue by trying to think of what you would say about the letters C and D. For example:

Clever C, can't find me.
Dandy D, I'm in a ditch.

Some of the children will be able to think of rhyming words and refrains for other letters.
Remember, the sillier the better! Don't try for all 26 letters,
just encourage the children to do the ones they know.

Name Bag

Materials
Index cards
Pen
Fancy or decorated bag (see Poetry Bag on page 111)

Write each child's name on a separate index card. Put the cards into the Poetry Bag.
Ask older children to pick names from the bag.
Encourage the children to make up rhymes about the names,
modeled after *An Edward Lear Alphabet* by Edward Lear, using one name at a time.
For example, if someone pulls out Claire's name from the bag,
the class might come up with this rhyme:
"C was once a little Claire.
Beary, Scary, Wary, little Claire."
If someone pulls out Alberto's name, they might make up this rhyme:
"A was once a little Alberto.
Loberto, Talberto, where is handsome Alberto?"
When a child's name is pulled from the bag, do not put it back in. This way, you can be sure that
all the children's names are pulled over a period of wait times.

Poems for Naptime

Materials

Book of poems, such as *Why Cowboys Sleep With Their Boots On* by Laurie Lazzaro Knowlton, or a Mother Goose book

Children fall in love with the sounds and patterns of the language of poetry. Whether it's modern poetry or from a long time ago, there's a poem that's just right for any transition.
If the children are getting ready for naptime, read "Wee Willie Winkie" from a Mother Goose book or a poem from *Why Cowboys Sleep With Their Boots On* by Laurie Lazzaro Knowlton.
Read the poem that begins:

Asleep a lot
Is good to be
When you are one, two or three.

Or you could recite:

To Bed

"Come, let's to bed," says sleepy head.
"Tarry awhile," says slow.
"Put on the pan," says Greedy Nan,
"We'll sup before we go."

What do the words *tarry* and *sup* mean? To help the children understand what they mean, use them in context. For example, "Don't tarry now, it's time to go out to play."
Or when it's time to eat, say, "Let's sup."
You also might want to recite some nursery rhymes, such as:

Bedtime

The man in the moon looked
Out of the moon,
Looked out of the moon and said,
"'Tis time for all children
On the earth
To think about getting to bed!"

Change the poem, substituting names of the children and teachers in the preschool. For example, "Sabrina looked out of the window and said, 'It's time for all children to go to bed.'"
Encourage the children to make up other names and places to replace the man in the moon.

Poems for Cleanup Time

Materials
None needed

Make clean-up time more fun with singing! Use the tune and phrasing from the song,
"Picking up paw paws, put them in a basket,
Picking up paw paws, put them in a basket."
However, sing or chant the words, "Picking up blocks, put them on the shelf," or
"Picking up games, put them in the game box," and so on.

Poems for Lunch or Snack

Materials
Books of poetry, such as *When We Were Very Young* by A. A. Milne
Butter, crackers, and marmalade, optional
Chart paper and marker, optional

If it's time for lunch or snack and the children have to wait for others to wash up,
read A. A. Milne's "The King's Breakfast" in *When We Were Very Young*.
In this poem, the king demands butter for his breakfast, but the cow says,
"Not now," and tells the king, "Many people nowadays like marmalade instead."
What do the children think? Do they like marmalade better than butter on their bread?
Have they tasted marmalade?

If desired, serve butter, crackers, and marmalade for snack later in the day
or the next day and recite the poem again.
Encourage the children to taste both the marmalade and the butter and decide which they prefer.
Count how many children like marmalade and
how many like butter to find out the most popular food.
Make a graph of the results (see example below).

I like marmalade	I like butter

From the same book, read, "Rice Pudding," which is a poem
about a girl named Mary Jane who won't eat rice pudding.
Encourage the children to talk about their favorite and least favorite foods.
Make a list of their choices.
Ask the children whether or not Mary Jane behaved appropriately in the poem.
Ask them what they would do or say if they really did not like a specific food.

Enchanting Sounds

Materials
Books of poetry (see suggestions below)

No matter how great a teacher you are and how carefully you've planned
to avoid making children wait, there will be times that, for one reason or another,
you'll have to wait. It doesn't matter, though.
There are plenty of poems that will not only fill time,
but will also fill the children's minds with the enchanting sounds of language.
The poems of John Ciardi, Shel Silverstein, and Jack Prelutsky are great
for waiting times or any other time of the day.
For example, the poem, "Mummy Slept Late and Daddy Fixed Breakfast"
from John Ciardi's *You Read to Me, I'll Read to You* is great for children of all ages.
It is about a daddy making waffles that look like manhole covers.

It ends with the child saying, "I think I'll skip the waffles."
Shel Silverstein's poetry is well known and liked by children. Read selections from
Where the Sidewalk Ends or any of his other books.
Jack Preltusky's poems, such as those in his book *It's Raining Pigs & Noodles: Poems,*
frequently use the repetition of the long *e* sound. You could use some of these poems to inspire
the children to make up chains of other words that rhyme.
Start a class poem. Begin with the phrase, "Never touch a monkey…,"
and ask the children to find other words that rhyme with monkey.

Connecting Home and School

Make copies of the poems and rhymes the children have enjoyed (including the poetry you and the children have created). Staple the pages between two sheets of construction paper and title it "Poems We Know." Encourage the children to share them with their families.

Mathematical Children

"I'm three-and-a-half," Molly tells a neighbor, "And my twin Monica is three-and-a-half, too!" she continues. Children, even before the age of three, use mathematics. They count, use measurement, and want the "biggest" cookie or "more" blocks. In preschool, children's everyday mathematical knowledge is extended, expanded, and clarified through meaningful, hands-on experiences. However, research also shows that children must practice and use the knowledge gained through first-hand experiences in order to learn mathematics concepts and skills. When you and the children have a wait time, use some of the following games and poems to pass the time while reinforcing and practicing content from the field of mathematics.

Measurement Game—Big-Little

Materials
Objects of different sizes

Focus the games you select around the National Council of
Teachers of Mathematics Standards (1998).
If your goal is to reinforce children's understanding of measurement,
do this activity or one of the following two activities.
Hold up a book or some other object and ask the children to find another object in the room that
is the same size as the book, one that is smaller, and one that is larger.
Continue by picking other objects and asking different children to find things in the room
that are just as tall as the object, taller, or shorter. Or, ask a child to find something in the room
that is as tall as she is, shorter than she is, and taller than she is.
Encourage the children to check their observations by placing
one object beside or on top of the other.
Vary the game to use other mathematical ideas and vocabulary.
For example, if the children are learning to use the terms "more than" or "less than," ask them to
find a plant in the room that has "more than" four leaves, someone who is wearing a piece of
clothing with "less than" four buttons, or a shelf with "more than" eight objects.

Measurement Game—Unit Blocks

Materials
Unit blocks
Chart paper and marker

Measure the children's feet, hands, legs,
or arms with unit blocks.
Find out how many blocks equal the length
of a child's foot or hand.
Stack blocks to see how many it takes
to equal the length of a child's leg.
Encourage the children to take turns
being measured and record your findings.

117

Follow up by asking the children the following riddle ("A Star"):

Higher than a house
Higher than a tree.
Oh! Whatever can that be?

As the children guess the things they think are higher than a house or tree,
list them on a chart. Then tell them what you think is the answer.
Encourage four- and five-year-olds to make up their own riddles. Ask them to think of an object
and then think of things that are smaller, taller, or wider than it.
For example:
Smaller than an ant
Smaller than a worm.
Oh! What can it be?
(A grain of sand)

Measurement Books

Materials
Books about measurement, such as *Perro Grande...Perro Pequeno* by P. D. Eastman, *The Little Red
Ant and the Great Big Crumb: A Mexican Fable* by Shirley Climo,
and *Big & Little* by Steve Jenkins

Extend the children's understanding of measurement by reading books such as *Perro Grande...Perro
Pequeno* by P. D. Eastman. This picture book about big and little dogs is written in Spanish and
English and introduces children to measurement.
Or, you could read *The Little Red Ant and the Great Big Crumb: A Mexican Fable*
by Shirley Climo, the story of ant that conquers all.
Big & Little by Steve Jenkins is a picture book pointing out the differences
in size between animals that are similar in other ways.
With the children, make up your own story of big and little.

Number Sense and Numeration— Mystery Bag

Materials
Bag or box
Objects from the classroom

If your goal is to increase the children's understanding of number sense and numeration, do this
activity or one of the following four activities.
Make a mystery bag or box and place a number of objects into it.
Ask a child to reach into the bag and, without looking, count the number of objects.
Then, ask her to take each object out of the box and count them.
Ask the children to hide their eyes while you increase or decrease the number of things in the bag.
Then, choose another child to count the objects.

Number Sense and Numeration— Count the Children

Materials
Chart paper and marker, optional

This rote counting activity is just fine to fill a few moments of wait time.
Encourage the children to count the number of children in the group; the number of boys and
the number of girls; how many are wearing something red, blue, yellow or orange; how many are
wearing shoes that tie, close with Velcro, slip on, or buckle.
If you have time, make a chart or graph of the children's findings.

Number Sense and Numeration— Count the Moves

Materials
Chart paper and marker

Ask each child to find her own space somewhere in the room.
Ask the children how many times they can:
★ hop on one foot
★ hop on the other foot
★ snap their fingers
★ jump on both feet
Encourage the children to tell the others how many times they were able to do each movement.
Record their names and the number on a chart.
Without drawing comparisons or using the numbers to ridicule children,
find the highest number of times the children could complete the tasks.

Number Sense and Numeration— A Counting Game

Materials
None needed

Ask each child to find her own space somewhere in the room.
While the children are in their spaces, play "Simon Says" as a counting game.
Use counting in the commands. For example, say, "Simon says take two steps forward."
"Take two steps to the side."
Catch children who do something without listening for the command, "Simon Says."
However, don't ask them to step out of the game because then
they would be waiting around instead of learning.

Number Sense and Numeration— Japanese Folk Game

Materials
None needed

Teach the children the Japanese folk game, "In a Spider's Web."
Encourage the children to make a "chain of elephants" by holding hands and walking around.
Choose one child to be the first elephant who gets caught in a spider's web.
Feeling lonely, the elephant selects another child to join her. Chant:

In a spider's web,
One elephant was hung.
She was lonely there,
So she called another one to come.

Then, sing or chant:

In a spider's web,
Two elephants were hung.
They were lonely there,
So they called another one to come.

This time, the second elephant picks another child to join them.
Play until all of the children are "hanging in the web."

Number Sense and Numeration— Fingerplays

Materials
None needed

Don't forget the fingerplays that involve children in counting and concepts of numeration.
You can use fingerplays in several ways:
★ teach children the motions they can make with their hands and fingers as they recite the rhyme.
★ use flannel board cutouts representing the animals, things, or characters in the fingerplay.
Give these to the children so they can place them on the flannel board as they occur in the rhyme.
★ encourage the children to reenact the rhyme themselves.

For example, play "Five Little Speckled Frogs."
(Or ten, depending on the age and experience of the children.)

Five Little Speckled Frogs

Five little speckled frogs
Living on a speckled log,
Eating a most delicious lunch.
One jumped into the pool,
Where it was nice and cool.
Now there are four little speckled frogs.
(Continue until there are no little speckled frogs left.)

First, show the children how to use their hands to be the frogs jumping in a pool.
Or make cutouts of frogs and ask the children to place them on a flannel board log.
Encourage the children to act out the fingerplay. If desired, ask the children who are wearing something speckled to be the frogs.
When the first group of five "frogs" is finished,
each child chooses another "frog" to take her place.

Another example is "Joan or Johnny Works With One Hammer."

Johnny Works With One Hammer

Johnny works with one hammer
One hammer, one hammer.
Johnny works with one hammer,
Then he works with two.

Continue until you get up to five hammers. The ending verse is:

Johnny works with five hammers,
Five hammers, five hammers.
Johnny works with five hammers,
Then he goes to sleep.

As you chant each verse, the children act out the movements.
First they make a fist and pound one knee (one hammer), then they make two fists and pound both knees (two hammers). For three hammers, they pound their knees with both fists and the floor with one foot, then both fists and both feet for four hammers.
For five hammers, they add the movement of shaking their heads back and forth.
A final example is "One to Ten." Ask the children to use their fingers
as counters as you recite the following nursery rhyme.

1, 2, 3, 4, 5
I caught a hare alive.
6, 7, 8, 9 10
I let it go again.

Ask the children if they know what a hare is. Tell them what it is (if needed).
Encourage the children to name another animal they could catch and repeat the rhyme.

Geometry and Spatial Sense—I Spy

Materials
Poems of Childhood
Gingham and calico fabric

If your goal is to foster the children's sense of geometry and spatial sense,
then do one of the following three activities.
Play "I Spy." Begin by saying, "I spy with my little eye something
red, round, and larger than an apple. What is it?"
Ask the children to guess what it is.
Encourage the children to take turns spying something and describing its shape, size, and color.
Look for shapes on the children's clothing.
Read Eugene Field's "The Duel" from *Poems of Childhood,* which is about a gingham dog and
calico cat. Show the children pieces of gingham and calico.
Then ask the children to look at the clothing they are wearing and identify shapes.
For example, the eyelets in their shoes are round, some buttons are square, and some of their
clothing may have stripes, circles, or other geometric shapes.

123

Geometry and Spatial Sense—Books

Materials
Books about shapes (see suggestions below)

Read *Pancakes, Crackers and Pizza: A Book About Shapes* by Marjorie Eberts to the children.
Encourage them to talk about the shapes of their favorite foods.
Read *Shapes, Shapes, Shapes* by Tana Hoban, which has photographs
of familiar objects such as a chair, barrettes, and a manhole cover.
This book encourages children to look at the world in a different way.
After you read the book, ask the children to explore their room
and find shapes that are not immediately recognizable in everyday objects.

Geometry and Spatial Sense—Mystery Bag

Materials
Bag or box
Parquetry blocks

Fill a mystery bag or box with different shapes of parquetry blocks.
Ask one child to pull out a block and ask the others to identify its shape.
Over time, make sure that each child has a chance to pull a block from the bag.
Use the bag of shapes again. This time, ask a child to pull out a shape and then find something
else in the room that is the same shape.

Estimation

Materials
Marbles
Small jar
Paper and marker
Timer or hourglass

If your goal is to foster the children's estimation skills, then:
★ Ask the children to estimate the number of marbles that will fit inside a small jar (one that holds fewer than a dozen marbles). Record their estimates. When the jar is about half full, ask them if they want to change their estimates.
Record the actual number.
★ Continue estimating by asking the children
how many steps it will take to walk across
the front of the room. Record their estimates and
then have a team of children walk across the room while the others count.
Record both the estimate and actual number.
★ Set a kitchen timer or use an hourglass to estimate how long the children will have to wait for something (for example, a classroom visitor, lunch, and so on).

Laughing, Joyous Children

Reading Silly Books

Materials
Silly books (see suggestions below)

What better time to lighten up and just have fun than when you have to wait?
Why not try reading silly books?
Pick books that are silly and take only a few minutes to read,
or those that can be stopped without really interrupting the story. Examples are:
★ *Jamberry* by Bruce Degen. "Rassberry, Jazzberry, Razzmattazzberry, Berry Band" and other rhymes in this book about the land of berries will delight children. It's pure fun!
★ Read *Miss Mary Mack: A Hand-Clapping Rhyme* by Mary Ann Hoberman.
Then, teach the children the hand rhyme, "Miss Mary Mack, Mack."
★ Read *Imogene's Antlers* by David Small, the story of a girl
who wakes up one morning with antlers.
Or read any other silly book and talk about the difference between make-believe and fact.

Play Silly Games—Keep the Basket Full

Materials
Large basket
Balls

Play "Keep the Basket Full."
Fill a large basket with a bunch of balls.
Ask the children to sit in a circle and choose one child to be the leader.
The leader counts the balls and then dumps the basket, making the balls roll all over.
The other children get up and capture as many balls as they can,
then bring them back to the basket.
The leader selects a new leader who counts the balls and begins the game again.

Play Silly Games—Rag Dolls

Materials
None needed

Ask the children to find their own space.
Encourage the children to pretend to be rag dolls.
Ask them to be very loose, like they don't have any bones to hold them up.
First they can droop their arms, then their head, chest, legs,
and body until they're all collapsed on the floor.

Play Silly Games—Wiggle Game

Materials
None needed

Ask the children to find their private space to play the wiggle game.
Start the game by saying, "My fingers are starting to wiggle, my fingers are starting to wiggle."
As you say this, everybody wiggles their fingers.
Proceed with wiggling the hands, feet, legs, and head—
until everyone's whole bodies are wiggling.
When everyone is full of giggles instead of wiggles, it is time to stop the game.

Play Silly Games—A Tapping Game

Materials
Drum, table, or floor
Rhythm sticks

Try a tapping game. Start by tapping a simple rhythm on a drum.
Encourage the children to copy the rhythm by tapping on their knees, tabletop, or floor.
Beat more sophisticated rhythms as the children copy them.
Ask the children to take turns playing the lead rhythm on the drum.
Use the tapping game to tap out the syllables in children's names.
For example, beat Al-bert-to, Sa-bri-na, Bry-an, Kim-ber-ly.

Sing Silly Songs and Chants

Materials
None needed

Enjoy one of these silly chants.

A Young Woman of Leeds (unknown)
There was a young woman of Leeds,
Who swallowed six packets of seeds.
It soon came to pass
She was covered with grass,
And couldn't sit down for the weeds.

Old Man of Peru (unknown)
There was an old man of Peru
Who dreamed he was eating his shoe.
He woke in the night
In a terrible fright,
And found it was perfectly true.

What Did You Do When You Had to Wait?

Assessing and Evaluating

What Did the Children Learn?

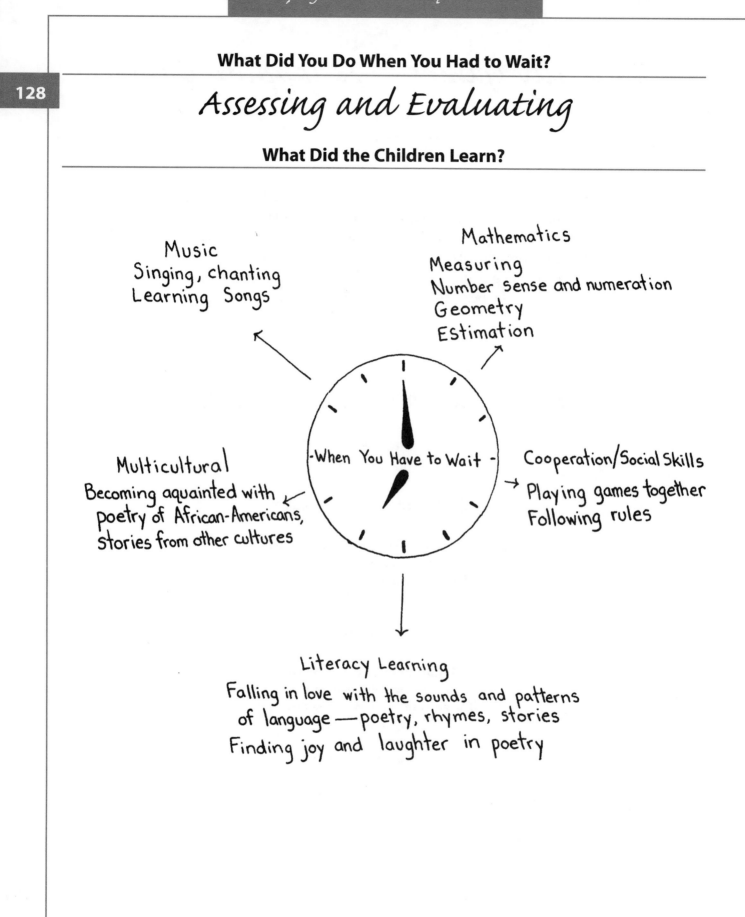

Music
Singing, chanting
Learning Songs

Mathematics
Measuring
Number sense and numeration
Geometry
Estimation

-When You Have to Wait-

Multicultural
Becoming aquainted with
poetry of African-Americans,
Stories from other cultures

Cooperation/Social Skills
Playing games together
Following rules

Literacy Learning
Falling in love with the sounds and patterns
of language — poetry, rhymes, stories
Finding joy and laughter in poetry

CHAPTER 6

Playing to Learn When Things Go Wrong

"I don't ever want to leave," said three-year-old Rachel after her first day in child care.
"I want to play here forever and ever." Quality child care programs, Head Start, and other preschool settings
are pleasurable places for children. When children are in an environment specifically arranged to meet
their physical, social, emotional, and cognitive needs, things rarely go wrong.
In good programs for young children, few problems arise. And, the few problems that do
are fleeting and easily solved with a change of pace, a smile, hug, or happy song.

But even in the best environments and programs, things can and do go wrong.
For example, some children may find the transition from home to the program difficult.
Others may have trouble adjusting to the group, or making and keeping friends.

Then there are days when everything seems to go wrong. The plans you've carefully made "bomb"
and things just get out of hand. Children start squabbling and fighting, not just with each other
but also with themselves! They express strong feelings—anger, frustration, and fears—in strong ways.
The peaceful learning setting you usually experience seems like a distant dream.

At other times, serious life events will affect you and the children. Illness occurs; divorces take place.
Tragedies happen—children or their families are in accidents, homes burn, and death occurs.
Even tragic events in the community or far from the children's here-and-now world affect them.
While they may not be directly involved in these events, the children still search for understanding.
"Will I get bombed?" "Why did she get shot?" "Will that hurricane get me?" It's up to you and family members
to help children accept and handle the resultant feelings and emotions.

This chapter offers teachers of young children ways to address and handle troubling times and events.
It suggests many things to do, including helping:
★ children make the transition to the child care center
★ children make and keep friends
★ guide children's behaviors
★ children cope with life's events, both near to them and far away

The suggestions and ideas in this chapter will guide you in developing
additional strategies for helping children adjust to their new setting, make friends,
handle behavior problems, and deal with difficult life events.

Children Make Transitions

"Okay. I know I won't like it, but I'll go just this once," says four-year-old Casey on the first day of preschool. Everyone feels a bit anxious when entering a group for the first time. Think about the first time you attended a workshop, support group, or new church by yourself. How did you feel? Did you wonder how you would be greeted? If you were wearing the right clothes? Would you know what to do?

Children have the same anxieties when they enter a new preschool or child care setting, only more so because their anxieties are complicated by their preoperational thinking. Their immature thinking leads them to worry that if their mother leaves, she won't be able to find them when it's time to go home. Or they may become frightened by even more irrational thoughts. One crying child finally was able to stop crying enough to tell the teacher, "There isn't a bedroom. If I have to stay here, where will I sleep?"

Some things you can do to ease children's worries and anxieties before they enter the group for the first time are:

★ *Planning one, two, or more visits with the parents to the center.*

Or, arrange for the child to visit with an older friend who once attended the center.

★ *Visiting the children in their homes before they come to the center. Bring along a photo album of children working and playing in the center. Together you and the child can "read" the book, talking about what he will do at the center.*

★ *Creating a website revolving around the center or school. Children and their families can view and read about what happens in the center. Post the calendar, a daily schedule, what children should wear, and a sample day.*

Connecting Home and School

Send parents a form to fill out for a library card from the local library. Attach a list of books they might find useful to read to their children to help them ease their transition to school. You might want to include:

★ *At Preschool With Teddy Bear* by Jacqueline McQuade, the story of Teddy Bear's first day at school.

★ *Will I Have a Friend?* by Miriam Cohen is a gentle story of how making a friend solves a child's anxieties about kindergarten.

★ *My First Day of School* by P.K. Hallinan traces a typical first day of school in a reassuring way.

Send a letter to each child welcoming him to the center. Include information about when class will begin and what, if anything, the child needs to bring to the center. Photographs of the center and classroom would also be helpful. Enclose a self-addressed envelope, and ask the child to dictate or write the things he wants to do and learn at the center. Ask the family to include a photo of the child.

When School Begins

Materials
Photographs of the children
Poster board
Tape or glue
Marker

Before school begins, tape or glue the children's photos you received to a piece of poster board.
Write the children's names under their photos.
When the children come to school, read out loud the list of things
they said they wanted to learn and do.
Write each child's ideas in a bubble above the child's photo.
Talk about how the children will have the opportunity to do the things they want. (One teacher
listed each of the things children wanted to learn on a 3" x 5" card. As she read the cards and
talked about what the children wanted to learn, she categorized their ideas, making a graph of the
cards. Then she summarized what the children would do and learn while in school.)

Transitioning to School

Materials
None needed

It may take a while before a child feels comfortable and begins playing with others.
If necessary, ask a parent or other family member to stay with the child. Give the children and their families plenty of time to adjust.
If the children are still hesitant or fearful of being away from their families for the first time or in a strange setting, accept their feelings. You might say, "I understand. It takes time to get used to a new place and children and people you don't know."
Refer to the children's parents during the day, reminding them that their parent is at work or at home and will be there to pick them up after nap, lunch, or playtime.

Say Hello

Materials
None needed

Children will enter and leave the group throughout the year. Encourage the children to welcome the new children to the group and say good-bye to those who leave.
When a new child enters the group, you can:
★ form a committee to show the child around the room and familiarize him with the center.
New children will want to know where the bathroom is,
how things work, and where they will keep their coats.
★ take the child on a tour of the center. Visit the director or principal's office, the cafeteria, and other classrooms to meet the teachers and children.
★ make a nametag for the child and read the child's name to the rest of the children.
Then ask the other children to put on their nametags and read their names out loud.
★ take a Polaroid photo of the child, label it with his name, and post it on a chart titled, "Welcome (Name of Child)." Read it to the children.

Connecting Home and School

Create a class book for the child to take home. Title it "Welcome to (the name of the room or class.)" Ask each child to draw or write about something they like to do when in the group. Help them sign their names.

Make a Welcome Chart

Materials
Photographs of children
Glue or tape
Mural paper
Markers

Ask each family to bring in a family photograph.
Glue or tape the photos on a piece of mural paper.
Under each photo, list:
★ names of the family members and pets
★ where the family lives
★ what they like to do
Read the chart to the class.
When the new child feels comfortable, encourage him to tell
the rest of the group about his family and life.

Saying Good-Bye

Materials
Books about saying good-bye (see suggestions below)

Just as new children will enter the group, others will move away and leave.
It's easy to feel sad and blue when a friend moves away.
Young children often do not understand what has happened when a child they knew and played
with fails to return. They may think that if they do something wrong, they also may disappear.

Plan ways to help the child who is leaving and the group say good-bye, such as:

★ Sing "Make new friends, but keep the old. One is silver and the other gold!" It tells the children that friends stay friends even though one may move away.

★ Read *Annie Bananie* by Leah Komaiko to the children. This is a story about a girl who is sad when her best friend moves away.

Friends Book

Materials
Standing mirror
Paper
Crayons or markers
Stapler
Construction paper

Make a "Best Friends" book for a child who is leaving.
Ask each child to draw a self-portrait and write or dictate a story about the fun they had together.
Set up a self-portrait table with a standing mirror, markers or crayons, and paper.
This way, the children can actually look at themselves as they draw.
Encourage the children to look at the shape and color of their eyes, eyebrows, eyelashes, nose, mouth, chin, cheeks, neck, and ears.
Staple together all the pages between two pieces of construction paper.

135

Good-Bye Book

Materials
Good-Bye, House by Robin Ballard
Paper, crayons, stapler, and construction paper

Read *Good-Bye, House,* about a child who says good-bye to her favorite places in her house. Ask the child who is leaving to make a "Good-Bye Center" book by drawing the places he will miss the most. Staple together the pages between two pieces of construction paper. He can leave the book with the group or take it with him. Set up an email system so children can draw or write letters to one another after the child has moved away.

Children Make and Keep Friends

When the children have adjusted to the new situation, it's time for them to make new friends. Some children do this naturally, with enviable ease. Others, however, need help making and keeping friends.

Helping Children Make Friends

Materials
None needed

To help children make friends, you might:
★ Make sure you call all the children by their names. Greet the children using name songs. Substitute children's names for those in songs and stories.
★ Organize a special playgroup of children who are very socially skilled with those who need to develop skills. For example, you could ask Andrea and Juan, who are highly sociable, to work with Jeanna at the water table or to build with the blocks.
★ Pair a very shy child with a younger child. Ask the shy child to help the younger child complete a puzzle, use the computer, or draw on the overhead.
★ Steer a child who has trouble entering a group to a smaller or more accepting group of children. Rather than suggesting the child attempt to enter on-going play by asking, "Can I play?" encourage him to observe a group, try to figure out the theme, and then think of a role that would contribute to the theme (Hazen, Black & Fleming-Johnson, 1984). For example, tell him, "Look, they're playing hardware store. You could be the cashier."
★ Create a group to complete a special task. With the aid of an assistant, select a group of children to plant seeds in the garden, go to buy fish for the aquarium, or create a puppet show.

Highlight the Skills of Children

Materials
None needed

Bring status and recognition to children who need help making friends. You might:
★ Ask the children who need recognition to demonstrate how they solved a problem or completed a puzzle. For example, "Kathy, show the group how you found 'Draw It' on the computer."
Or to a group who is sewing, say, "Alberto, will you help others knot the threads?"
★ Ask the child to carry the flag in a marching band
and then choose the next child to carry the flag.
★ Pick the child to be Simon and lead the others in playing "Simon Says."
Or ask him to be the first duck when playing "Duck, Duck, Goose!"
★ Sing songs that foster interaction with others.
For example, "If you're happy and you know it, hug a friend…, …give them five," and so on.

Guiding Children

Materials
None needed

Direct guidance is another way of helping children make friends and gain acceptance. This includes:
★ On the spot, help the children negotiate with others. For example, "Tell her you don't want to be the baby, but you would like to be the Auntie," or "When you talk to him, look at him. Then he'll know you want him to listen."
★ Challenge the children if they call one another names. "You hurt Joel's feelings when you called him a meanie. What did you really want to say to him?"
Encourage the child to think of other interpretations of the event.
★ Intervene when a child is having difficulty with others by making suggestions in experimental form. For example, "Have you tried…?" "Try doing… If it doesn't work, come back and we'll think of something else to try."

Sock Puppets

Materials
Socks
Glue
Markers and other decorating materials

Make a couple of sock puppets to teach the children social skills.
Draw or glue decorating materials to the socks to make animal characters.
Use the puppets to act out situations and solve problems. For example, the two puppets both
want to play with the same toy. They tug, pull, hit, and fight, saying, "It's mine! It's mine!"
Ask the children, "What should they do?" Encourage the children
to help the puppets solve the problem.
Ask the children to take turns being the puppets and solving the problem.

Books About Social Skills

Materials
Books about social skills (see suggestions below)

Use children's literature as a springboard for talking about social skills.
Read the children *Let's Be Enemies* by Janice Udry. In the book, one boy says that James used to
be his friend but now he's an enemy. He describes what James did to him,
such as throwing sand, being the boss, and so on.
You might stop reading and ask the children if this has ever happened to them, why they think
James is acting the way he is, and what they would do about it.
Another good book to read is *The Berenstain Bears and the Trouble With Friends* by Stan & Jan
Berenstain. Even though the Berenstain Bears may seem gender-biased, children adore the book's
understandable, simple morals of learning that they can't be friends and both have their own way.

Making Friends With Children Who Have Special Needs

Children with special needs like to have friends, too. Help the children accept and make friends with others who have special needs. Some ways to do this are:

★ modeling how to help the child with special needs. For example, give short explanations as you hand the child her crutches, "Saundra needs her crutches now," or as you put things in her backpack, "Saundra can carry this in her backpack."

★ teaching the children to persevere when interacting with a child with disabilities. For example, waiting for the child to respond and interact, looking directly at a hearing-impaired child when speaking, or holding the arm of a visually impaired child when walking to the play yard.

★ making certain the child with special needs is fully included. If a child is in a wheelchair, for example, ask all the children to sit on chairs during circle or story time so they are the same height as the child in the chair. Or if feasible, provide scooter boards for physically disabled children to use to scoot around the room or play yard.

★ making sand and water tables accessible to all the children.

★ providing materials that encourage social interaction, such as matching toys and materials that require more than one child to complete.

★ encouraging the children to spend time with a child with special needs by asking them to work with him. Reinforce their behavior by recognizing their social abilities.

Guiding Children's Behaviors When Groups Get Out of Hand

What happened? You made the best of plans. You put out fresh pans of paint on a table top, you welcomed each child with a song as he arrived, and you had a row of frogs that you'd spent the previous night making lined up for the children to play with on the flannel board. But nothing went as planned. Instead of peacefully painting, the children began splashing paint on one another. Instead of putting frogs on the flannel board, a couple of children started chasing each other around, trying to put frogs on each other's heads. When two children bumped into each other, the tears, screaming, and chaos began in full. What do you do now?

Speak Softly

Materials
None needed

Sit on a small chair in the circle area and in a soft, very soothing voice, call the children to join you. All you need to begin is one or two children to draw the others to you.
Continue talking in a low, soft, calming voice so the children
will want to hear what you are saying.
When all the children are together, ask them to problem solve. Even two-year-olds can come up with solutions when asked, "What is happening here?" "What are we going to do about it?"

A Change of Pace

Materials
None needed

Try a change of pace.
Start singing a calming, familiar, well-loved song.
It might be as simple as, "Here we are together, together, together at school. We'll all learn to read, and we'll all learn to write...here we are together, together at school."

Turn It Off!

Materials
None needed

Reduce stimulation.
Turn off CD players and computers, and remove noisy toys.
Temporarily close off the areas where the trouble started, such as the Block or Housekeeping Areas.

Take a Break

Materials
None needed

Stop and take a break.
Call the children to you and ask them to stretch out their arms and legs, wiggle their heads, take deep breaths, and become as quiet as they can be.
Then, ask them to choose a quiet, restful activity. They may:
★ choose to lie on their cot and rest
★ take a pillow into the Library Area and read a book
★ "read" a book to a doll or stuffed toy in the Dramatic Play Area
★ string beads at a table
★ sit at a table and watch the sand fall in an hourglass, watch the fish in the aquarium, or uncover the ant farm and watch the ants working away
★ stretch out on the rug for a few minutes
★ listen to a story using a tape recorder
★ sit in the rocking chair

141

Quiet Activities

Materials
See suggestions below

Keep some quiet activities in reserve to bring out when the children need calming. For example:
★ Make a "dollhouse" out of a discarded bookshelf. Wallpaper different shelves using different types of paper. Add several wooden props, small dolls, and a few pieces of furniture and keep the dollhouse shelf turned to the wall, using the back as a place to display children's work. When things need calming down, turn the shelf around to entice quiet play.
★ One teacher kept a set of brightly colored plastic shapes that adhered to a plastic sheet. She brought these out as a choice when she sensed that children needed to quiet down.
★ Set up a table with clean shoestrings and small bowls of cereal, such as Cheerios, for children to eat, talk, and make strings of cereal.
★ Stop what you are doing and have a snack, even if it's not scheduled. Bring out cups, a pitcher of juice, and a plate of crackers. Sit together, relax, and talk about the day.

Analyze What Happened

Materials
None needed

After the children have calmed down and the immediate problem is solved, take time to analyze what happened: Ask yourself:
★ Did the children lose control because they were tired, exhausted, and needed to rest?
★ Were they in need of nutrition? Did they need something to eat or drink?
★ Were the activities scheduled beyond the children's abilities?
Were you introducing something they didn't need to know or learn at this time?
Perhaps something they would learn with ease later?
★ Did the children need to let off steam? Did you ask them to sit and be quiet for too long?
Did they need to run, jump, and release their pent-up energy?

Most times, with a well planned, balanced program, children manage to work together peacefully, solving problems and negotiating with others as needs arise. Within groups, however, there will be individual children who lose control, bully, tease, and lash out at others.

Helping Children Gain Control

Materials

None needed

Try one of the following steps to help individual children gain control:

★ Many children just need a look, raised eyes, or a shake of the head to remind them of how they are expected to behave.

★ If they don't respond, try a physical reminder. For example, a light hug, a touch on the shoulder, or holding a hand helps many children gain control.

★ Repeat the rules of behavior, in a matter-of-fact way. "Walk here," "Tell her what you want," or "No hitting."

★ Physically remove the child from the group, repeating the rules, "I cannot let you throw sand at others, and I will not let others throw sand at you." Then do some brainstorming with the child about why the situation occurred and what the child will do in the future.

Helping Aggressive Children

Materials

None needed

Is there a bully in the class? A teaser? A highly aggressive child? Here are some other things teachers have found successful in helping these children gain control. Keep in mind that children bully, tease, or act out for a reason. To help the bully or teaser:

★ Try to figure out why the child bullies others and teases. Research suggests that many children act aggressively toward others because they themselves feel insecure, anxious, and cautious.

★ If this is the case, make sure to give the bully a great deal of attention when he acts appropriately. Recognize the child when he is playing well with others by saying, "Good job!" or "You did that well—you asked her for the trike." Or show the group how the child completed a block building, helped another with a puzzle, and so on.

★ Make certain that the child experiences success. Give the bullying child tasks that are challenging, yet achievable. Offer guidance and support so he does succeed. "I'll hold this part so you can put the C-clamp on this side."

143

Observing an Aggressive Child

Materials

None needed

Many aggressive children bully, tease, or hurt others
because they feel helpless, powerless, and worthless.
If this is the case, do not let the child gain power or control by acting aggressively.
Observe the child or ask a volunteer to observe him.
By observing the child closely, you will see when he is ready to act out.
This will help you stop him from acting out.
Teach the other children to ignore the threats, shouts, or taunts of the bullying child.
Serve as a model and ignore threats directed toward you. Make statements such as,
"When Jamie calls you a crybaby, he's trying to make you cry. If you don't cry
and walk away, he'll stop. I'll be here, and I won't let him hurt you."

Working With an Aggressive Child

Materials

None needed

Help the aggressive child gain control.
Go over the choices for the day and help the child get organized.
Set up steps for the child to take when he thinks he may act out.
Teach the child to put whatever is in his hand down.
Suggest that the child take a breath before talking,
which helps with aggression and teaches social skills.

Children Cope With Life Events

Life events affect children. Friends or family become ill, parents get divorced, and tragedies occur near the children's homes and far away.

When children experience a life-changing event, whether it is an illness, a divorce in the family, violence and aggression, or some other disturbing life event, they will feel threatened, insecure, and frightened. Often, because of their immature thinking processes, they believe the event happened because they were bad, didn't obey their parents, or did something else that they should not have done.

Regardless of the event, young children need to know that they are safe, will be cared for and protected, and will be loved—no matter what. You can help by making certain that the children feel safe and secure.

Staying Calm

Materials
None needed

Children look to the adults around them for comfort and security.
They take their cues from you. If you are upset and frantic,
they will sense this and become frantic as well.
Whatever the event or situation, use a soft, quiet, and calming voice to assure the children that
they will be safe, protected, and loved.

Keeping Daily Routines the Same

Materials
None needed

No matter how much the world around the children changes, keeping the same
daily routines helps them feel a measure of security and protection.

145

Minimizing Stress

Materials

None needed

Avoid adult discussions and arguments in front of the children.
If parents are fighting, ask them to wait for you in the teachers' lounge or office.
Avoid teacher discussions of adult topics in front of children.

Observing and Listening to Children

Materials

None needed

Before talking with a child or group, try to find out what the children
are thinking and understanding about a troubling event.
Ask them, "Tell me what happened. What do you think about it?
Why do you think this happened? What do you think will happen now?"
Respond based on what the children already know. Clarify misconceptions, straighten out facts,
and reassure the child that he will be safe and protected.
News of violence, wars, bombings, hurricanes, tornadoes, killings, and other tragic events
reaches children on a daily basis. As with adults, children will question these events
and need help in understanding and coping with them.

Preparing for Discussion, Play, and Action

Materials

See suggestions below

Observe children at play and listen to what they are saying about an event.
Talk to them about it. You might want to take part of circle time
to discuss the event with the children.
For example, start by asking, "Did anyone see the tornado on television last night?"
Leave a long silence and let each child speak at length,
interrupting each other as they wish. You might:

★ List the children's comments on a chart as they talk.

★ Validate their feelings and ideas. (For example, "A lot of people feel that way.")

★ Tell them the factual version of what happened.

★ Recognize their emotions.

★ Keep repeating that the parents and adults who take care of them are doing everything they can to keep the children safe and protected.

★ Provide art materials and encourage the children to represent their ideas of the event or release their emotions.

★ Give the children props so they can play out their fears and ideas, and find emotional release.

★ Help them write letters to authorities about their ideas and feelings. They may want to write to the mayor, governor, Congressional representative, or President expressing their fears and concerns.

Connecting Home and School

When talking with the children about life's events, make certain that you:

★ Ask the parents their views and ideas of how you should talk to the children about the event.

★ Send a letter home to families telling them how you've handled the event at school, what you said and did, and how the children responded.

★ Offer suggestions and resources that the parents can use.

147

What Did You Do When Things Went Wrong?

Assessing and Evaluating

What Did the Children Learn?

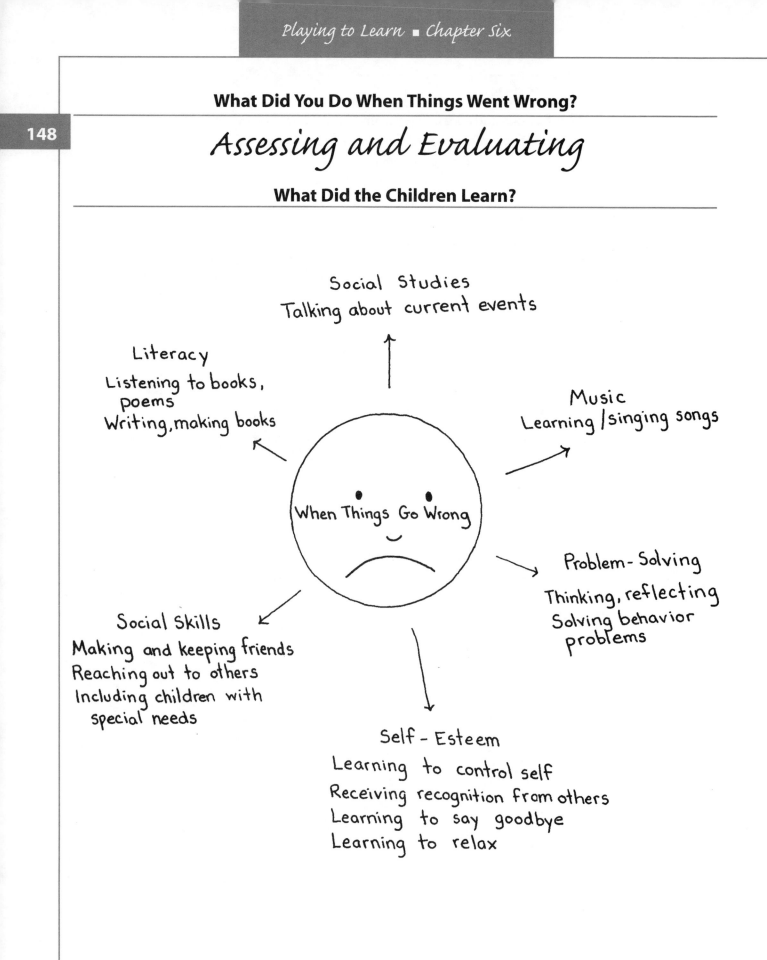

Social Studies
Talking about current events

Literacy
Listening to books,
  poems
Writing, making books

Music
Learning/singing songs

When Things Go Wrong

Problem-Solving
Thinking, reflecting
Solving behavior
  problems

Social Skills
Making and keeping friends
Reaching out to others
Including children with
  special needs

Self-Esteem
Learning to control self
Receiving recognition from others
Learning to say goodbye
Learning to relax

CHAPTER 7

Playing to Learn When Taking a Walk

"There's nothing to do," the children whine. Yes, there is—they can go on a walk! What could be better? Taking a walk refreshes the children physically, mentally, and emotionally. Walking gives everyone a change of pace, time to stretch and relax, and an opportunity to learn a myriad of things. As children walk through and around their school, around the block, and through their neighborhood, they are:

★ gaining observation skills

★ becoming familiar with their immediate social and physical world

★ developing concepts of their social, economic, and physical worlds

This chapter includes many ideas for fostering children's observational skills and offers guides to planning meaningful trips into the children's immediate communities. The suggested trips are designed to foster the children's ability to develop concepts from the social, economic, and physical sciences through observation. Keep in mind that they are only suggestions. Each school is different, and each neighborhood and community has different geographical features and social and economic institutions for children to explore.

Observing Children

Just like adults, children observe all the time. We look, listen, feel, and sense the environment around us. However, much of this observing is habitual and so automatic, it takes place without thought. But when we are faced with a new situation or when we want to learn more about a situation, our observing becomes more focused and we attend to things and our environment in a more intentional way.

Start by taking the children on walks through the center or school. The purposes of these walks include:

★ fostering the children's observation skills

★ familiarizing the children with the center, school, church, or other building in which their center is housed

★ developing their knowledge of what else takes place in the building where their space is located

★ building feelings of security and safety through knowledge of their space

★ introducing the children to their social world

Developing Observation Skills

Materials
Stand-up mirror
Paper
Markers
Stapler
Construction paper

Foster the children's abilities to observe using their eyes.
Ask them to examine their own eyes.
Place a stand-up mirror, paper, and markers on a table.
Encourage the children to look into the mirror and talk about their eyes.
Help them use words that describe the color and shape of their eyes.
Name the parts of the eye—pupil, whites, eyelashes, lids, and eyebrows.
Then, ask each child to draw, write, or dictate something about her eyes.
Staple together the pages between two pieces of construction paper
to make a class booklet. Title it, "Our Eyes."
Read the booklet to the children and keep it in the Library Area.

Animals' Eyes

Materials
Books with close-up pictures of animals

Encourage the children to look at the animals' eyes in the books.
Ask them where the eyes are on different animal's heads.
Some animals, such as dogs and cats, have eyes in the front of their face. Others, such as rabbits,
have eyes on the sides of their head so they have a wider field of vision and can see predators.

Look and Magnify

Materials
Magnifying glasses
Objects to view

Put magnifying glasses and things that children can examine
with the aid of magnification on a table.
Encourage them to use the glasses to look closely at the objects.
For example, if they look at a flower, they can see how petals are attached
to a flower or the tiny hairs that make a leaf feel fuzzy.

Viewing Tubes

Materials
Empty paper towel tubes
Paper
Paste or tape
Crayons or markers

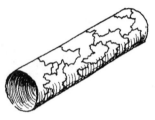

With children over the age of three, make "viewing tubes."
Collect a bunch of paper towel rolls and ask the children to decorate them.
They can paste or tape pieces of paper to the rolls and draw on them.
Go outside with the children and demonstrate how to view specific things
by looking through the tube with one eye.

A Circle of Yarn

Materials
Pieces of yarn, string, or rope
Clipboards, paper, and markers

An observation technique to use with children who are at least four years old is to give each child
a long piece of colored yarn, string, or rope; a clipboard with paper; and markers.
Ask the children to take the string outside, choose a place they want to observe,
and enclose the space with a circle of string.
Then, they can observe everything in their space and record their observations on the clipboard.
Instead of asking what they see or what they think, take your cues from the children—listen,
watch, share their interest, and delight in their findings.
Ask them questions that will help further their investigations (Dighee, 1998).
After they have finished, they can compare their observations.

Before Taking a Walk or Going on a Field Trip:

★ Give each child a clipboard, marker, and paper.

★ Agree ahead of time what the children are to observe.

★ Make up a list of questions that the children want to ask and write them on a chart. Go over the questions before the trip. Cut the list apart and give each child a question to ask.

★ If you are going to a factory or other place that has machines, divide the group into four groups. Ask each group to observe a specific thing. For example, ask one group to observe and record the machines that are used, another group to write down all the furniture they see, the third group to record all the signs they see, and the fourth group to write the names and draw pictures of people at work.

153

Start with the Familiar

Materials
Map of the building or school (or make one)
Sticky stars or stickers

With the children, consult a map of the building or school.
Put a star or sticker on the space representing your room.
Walk though the building with the children and refer to the corridors, stairs, or elevators you take and show the children how these are marked on the map.

Observing Shapes

Materials
Clipboards, paper, and markers

Give the children clipboards, markers, and a page that has columns
to record circles, squares, triangles, and other shapes.
Take a walk outside to identify the different shapes that can be found on the surface of the building, the sidewalks, driveways, or any other outdoor place.
When the children spy one of the shapes, they can sketch it on their clipboard.
Back in the classroom, encourage the children to discuss the shapes they saw.
Provide the children with opportunities to recreate the experience of their walk by building with blocks, creating shape designs with parquet blocks, constructing with empty boxes and other junk objects, or painting or drawing.

Observing People

Materials
None needed

Take the children on a walk around the building to observe people at work.
Find out where the janitor works, what she or he does, observe the tools he or she uses, where they are stored, and how they are used.
On another day, visit the school's office. Find out who works there and what they do.

If you have a cafeteria, visit the people who work there.
If your center is located in a temple or church, visit the sanctuary and ask
the rabbi, priest, or pastor to talk about what they do.
Many centers are located in the building where children's parents work. If this is the case,
plan trips to visit each child's parent at work.

Observing Older Children

Materials
Paper
Markers

With the children, observe older or younger children at play and work.
If your center is in an elementary school, for example,
ask the children what they think fifth graders do and learn.
Make a list of their ideas.
Then, help them write a letter to the fifth grade, asking if they can visit.
Fifth graders may be able to read to the children, show them displays of their work,
or explain how they do mathematics.

Observing Details

Materials
None needed

During various walks, encourage the children to focus on one of the following:
★ Find signs in the building. Read the signs that have words.
Ask them to count the signs they see without words.
★ On another day, walk through the building to find out what materials the school is made of.
What are the walls, windows, doors, and floors made of? What is the furniture made of?
★ Take a trip to count the number of doors on a given floor, the number of windows,
and the number of people who work in the office, cafeteria, or engineers' room.
★ Locate and record the address of the school. They might be able to find street signs
so they can see the names of the street.
★ Follow the path of the contents of the classroom trashcan as it goes from
the classroom to the custodian's room to the dumpster.

156

Observing Machines

Materials
None needed

One day, go on a "machine walk" to find
and name all of the machines used in the building.
Go to the office, cafeteria, and engineers' rooms.
Ask the workers to describe how they use
the copy machine, fax, phone,
computer, floor polisher, blender, beater, and other machines.
Children might take turns
handling the floor polisher, making copies,
or blending batter for biscuits.

A Studying Walk

Materials
Clipboards and paper
Markers
Rope or string

Divide the group into smaller groups and take a walk to study the play yard.
Assign the groups to:
★ Count the number of pieces of climbing equipment on the play yard.
★ Take a survey of all the children to find out their favorite piece of play yard equipment.
★ Use arbitrary measures (such as a piece of rope or string) to find out which piece is tallest.
★ Draw a map of the play yard.
★ Study the sand box. How big is it? They can use the rope again to measure the sand box.
Count the pieces of equipment in the sandbox.

Observing by Listening

Materials
Stand-up mirror
Paper
Markers or crayons
Books with close-up pictures of animals

Children learn about their world by listening as well as looking.
Repeat the eye activities, only this time focus on the ears.
★ Set up a table with a stand-up mirror and ask the children to observe the shape, size, and position of their ears. Ask them to draw their ears.
★ Encourage them to observe the animal's ears in the books. Which animals have the largest and smallest ears? Which animals have hidden ears? Or no ears at all?

Listening Game

Materials
Kitchen timer

Play a listening game to focus the children's attention on learning through listening.
Play "Where Is It?"
Set a kitchen timer for less than a minute.
Ask one to child hide the timer while the others cover their eyes.
When the timer goes off, ask the children to guess where it is hidden.
Make sure that each child, at one time or another, has a chance to hide the timer.

Guess What Is Inside

Materials
Empty plastic pill bottles or film canisters
Materials such as salt, sand, paper clips, uncooked rice, and so on
Opaque tape

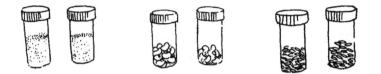

Montessori designed a series of wooden cylinders, all the same size, with various materials enclosed inside each one. He made matching pairs using sand, salt, pebbles, dried beans, and metal pins. The object was for the children to develop
the ability to match the containers holding the same type of material.
Replicate Montessori's original sound makers by filling pill bottles
or film canisters with various materials. Make sets of two using salt,
paper clips, uncooked rice, and anything else that will make a sound when shaken.
Securely tape the lids onto the bottles and cover the outside with opaque tape as well. Encourage the children to match the bottles containing the same material by themselves or with partners.

Listening Walks

Materials
Clipboards, paper, and markers

Take the children for a walk through the building to listen to the sounds of the building.
Before you take the children, go by yourself on a walk so you know ahead of time what sounds the children might be able to hear and focus on, and when and where they occur.
Give the children clipboards, paper, and markers. Discuss the purpose of their walk
and ask them to listen for sounds of:
★ Shoes on different floor surfaces. Can they tell who is walking by listening to the sounds?
Listen to the clip of high heels, the thump of slip-ons or sandals, or the clump of workers' boots.
Ask the children to sketch the shoes they hear and see.
★ Children working. Ask the children to listen to the sounds coming from different classrooms and guess what the children inside are doing or if they are happy or sad. Go outside and listen to the sounds of children playing. Ask the children to describe the differences between
the sounds children make in their rooms and in the play yard.

★ School machines. Listen to the sound of a floor polisher or other tools the janitor uses, as well as office and cafeteria sounds. Ask the children to record these sounds by drawing pictures.

★ The school grounds. Knowing what sounds occur around the school makes it possible to take children to where sounds will likely happen, such as a garbage truck as it lifts the dumpster from the ground, or the cafeteria as older children practice for a music recital.

Read and Walk

Materials
Walk With Me by Naomi Danis

Read *Walk With Me* by Naomi Danis to the children.
This short, sweet story about a mother and child exploring the outdoors
can help focus the children's observations.

Sing and Walk

Materials
None needed

Take a walk around the building while singing or chanting the following:

Let's take a walk.
Let's take a walk.
We'll hop and glide
And stop to talk.
Let's take a walk.

As you walk around the building, ask the children to observe whatever interests them.
They may notice animal or plant life, other children, workers, trucks, cars, or other things you
hadn't thought would interest them.
Stop to talk about what they see and hear.

Walks Around the Neighborhood

Materials

One Afternoon by Yumi Heo, optional

Take walks around the neighborhood for the specific purpose of fostering
the children's ability to observe through listening.
Before going on the walk, read *One Afternoon* by Yumi Heo, if desired. It is a story about young
Minho and his mother going for an afternoon outing. As they run their errands, they discover
that every place has a special sound.
Take the children on a walk around the school's neighborhood to hunt for sounds.
They may not hear a Laundromat or an elevated train,
but every neighborhood has its unique sounds.

More Ideas for Listening Walks

Materials

None needed

On listening walks, you might:
★ Stop when you hear a specific and unique sound and ask the children to listen.
Perhaps you can hear a bird singing, workers hammering, or a wind chime clanging in the breeze.
Encourage them to tap out the rhythm of the workers, try to sing like the bird,
or wiggle and clang like the wind chime.
★ On another day, take a walk to listen to the sound of birds. Do all birds sing the same songs?
Listen to the birds in the play yard. How do their songs differ?
★ Bring a tape recorder on a sound hunt to record some of the sounds the children hear. Later,
back in the room, see if the children can identify the sounds on the tape recorder
and guess where they were at the time (Seefeldt & Galper, 2001).
★ Ask the children to listen to the sounds that are nearby and those that are far away.
For example, if they hear a siren in the distance, ask the children to follow the sound as it comes
closer to them. Ask how the sound changes as its source comes nearer. Do the same with the
sound of children's feet running in the play yard, airplanes, or birds (Seefeldt & Galper, 2001).

A Map of Our World

Materials
Paper
Markers
Sticky stars or stickers

Begin to acquaint the children with the social world of their building and immediate area.
Make a map of the building and the area just around the building.
Again, mark your room with a star.
Take a walk outside with the children, going just around the building.
On another day, take a walk outside the building and ask them to figure out where their room is in relation to their current position.
What other rooms can the children identify as they walk around the building?
Look at the map so they get used to locating themselves in space by reading maps.

Broadening Children's Horizons

Take the children on field trips away from school to broaden their horizons and introduce them to concepts of their social, economic, historical, and physical worlds. No matter where you live, many of these concepts can be studied right in your neighborhood. Take a ride around the school, making sure not to go further than walking distance for the children. Note any areas of interest or things children can study within this distance. You might note:

★ Types of housing and other buildings

★ Street signs

★ Plants, trees, and shrubs

★ Different types of pavement, cement, blacktop, and sand

★ Businesses

★ Parks and recreation areas

★ People at work, such as police officers, letter carriers, and construction workers

★ Libraries and other public facilities

★ Places of historic interest

Before Taking a Walk Off School Grounds

Before going on the walk, make certain you have:

★ Enough trained volunteers or staff with you to supervise and work with individual children or small groups of three or four children. Sometimes it's enough to meet with the volunteers and the children to discuss the rules that will be followed on a walking trip away from the school (for example, stay with the group; walk; do not cross streets without an adult; observe flowers, plants, and any animals using eyes and ears, rather than touch and smell; and so on). You may, however, want to reinforce the procedures and rules with the children and give the volunteers a written list.

★ A first-aid kit complete with salve for scrapes, bandages, and a list of the children and their up-to-date emergency phone numbers. Consult the list of children's allergies so you'll know which children are sensitive to certain animals, insect stings, and food.

★ Provisions, if necessary, for water, snack, bathroom needs, and rest.

★ Several maps of the area.

★ Arrangements with people you will visit. (Call ahead to the post office, florist, clothing store, church, gasoline station, and so on.)

★ Transportation if the place you want to visit is more than a mile away from the school. This involves making certain that each child has the appropriate permission and child seat or seat belt, and that the drivers are fully aware of their responsibility to manage the children while driving. Repeat the school's rules to drivers, such as no cell phone use, and so on.

Children's Social World

Materials
None needed

Young children can probably walk a mile (round trip) if they have plenty of rest stops and water. By walking a mile or so in the vicinity of the school, the children can be put in touch with any number of social institutions. You might want to:

★ Watch community workers, such as a letter carrier. Arrange with the letter carrier ahead of time to take a few moments to stop the truck, show the children the inside of it, and let them follow as he or she delivers mail. Next, take a trip to visit the post office.

★ Visit the local library and arrange for each child to receive a library card and check out a book or two to take home.

★ Take advantage of any repair work that takes place in your neighborhood. Find out what the workers are doing, observe how they are doing it, and talk to people (if they are willing) to find out more about their job.

★ Take a trip to your home. Children may think that you sleep at the school and may be very surprised to find out that you don't. (For example, after a snowstorm, one teacher took her class to her home to take a sled ride down the hill in her backyard; another made a picnic lunch for the children to eat under the trees in her yard.) Regardless, the children will be impressed to see your bed, bathroom, kitchen, and other rooms in your home.

If desired, read them *My Teacher Sleeps in School* by Leatie Weiss.

★ Stop to look at the flowers in a neighbor's yard. Ahead of time, ask the neighbor if she or he would talk with the children about growing flowers, and perhaps give each child a cutting or seeds to plant.

★ If your center is employer-sponsored, it may be possible to visit family members at work. Arrange ahead of time for the family member and supervisor to show the children things of interest to them.

163

*Playing to Learn
When Taking a Walk*

Children's Physical World

Materials
None needed

You might:
★ Take a walk to look at and name the different kinds of houses, such as duplexes, apartments, bungalows, or other types of homes.
★ Identify street signs and house numbers and talk about why street names and numbers are required.
★ Check a map you've drawn of the area, and ask the children to follow the map with you as you stop at intersections, identify landmarks, street signs, or landforms.
Every place is special. What makes the place where you and the children live special? Take a walk around the neighborhood to observe its special physical features. You might:
★ walk to a park and run up and down hills
★ feed ducks at a nearby pond
★ identify trees, plants, and animals that live around your school

Children's Economic World

Materials
None needed

Children's concepts of consuming and purchasing are immature, and will remain so for quite a few more years until they are nearly in the stage of formal thinking (around 11 or 12 years of age). Children may think that clothing and other goods are made at the back of a store, and they have no clear idea about the purpose of exchanging money to pay for things. Trips to stores and other businesses can begin to fulfill the children's need to know and help them begin to understand their economic world.
Since children may not know what happens in the back of a store, take them on "behind the counter" trips. You might:

★ Visit a gas station. Encourage the children to watch people pump gas and observe the repair shop. Watch cars go up and down the lift, ask the mechanics what they are doing and why, and check out the machinery.

★ Go behind the counter at the supermarket to the loading dock and watch workers unload fruit, vegetables, and other goods. However, do not ask the children to watch people unload sides of beef or other meat. Young children are appalled, and even frightened at the idea of meat coming from an actual animal.

★ Look in the back of a clothing store. Children may expect to see workers sewing jeans, but instead will be fascinated with the inventory and how it's managed.

Shopping Trips

Materials
Paper, and pen or marker

Go on specific shopping trips. For example, visit a nursery to buy plants for the school garden. Or, visit a home improvement store to purchase wood to make a rabbit hutch or shelf for the room.
Before you do go:
★ make a shopping list
★ determine how much you will spend
★ divide the children into groups and give each group a specific assignment (shop for potting soil, fertilizer, plants, potting tools, or a planter).

Trip to Pick Apples or Pumpkins

Materials
For three-year-olds:
Red, green, and yellow apples or pumpkins
Cutting board and knife (teacher only)
Red, green, and yellow paint
Paintbrushes
Paper

For four- and five-year-olds:
Same as for three-year-olds, plus plans for a field trip to an apple orchard or pumpkin patch
Apples and Pumpkins by Anne F. Rockwell

Three-year-olds do not need to take a field trip to pick apples. Instead, bring a bunch of red, green, and yellow apples or pumpkins to the center.
Encourage them to feel the apples.
Ask the children to sort the apples by color, feel, size, or by some other category that makes sense to them.
Peel an apple. How do they feel and look before they are peeled? After?
Cut open an apple and look at the seeds.
Slice apples for the children to eat.
Taste them and ask the children to decide which one they like best.
Give the children red, green, and yellow paint, brushes, and large paper to paint pictures with "apple colors."
For four- and five-year-olds, read *Apples and Pumpkins* by Anne F. Rockwell, the story of a family's journey to a farm to pick apples and pumpkins.
Before going to pick apples or pumpkins, bring several small pumpkins or different kinds of apples to the classroom.
Encourage the children to feel them, hold them, and carry them around.
Discuss the shape, color, and feel of the pumpkins.
Make plans for what kind of pumpkin they'll purchase at the farm.
Determine how much money each child will have to spend, and how many and what size pumpkins or apples they can buy with the money.

Assessing and Evaluating

What Did the Children Learn?

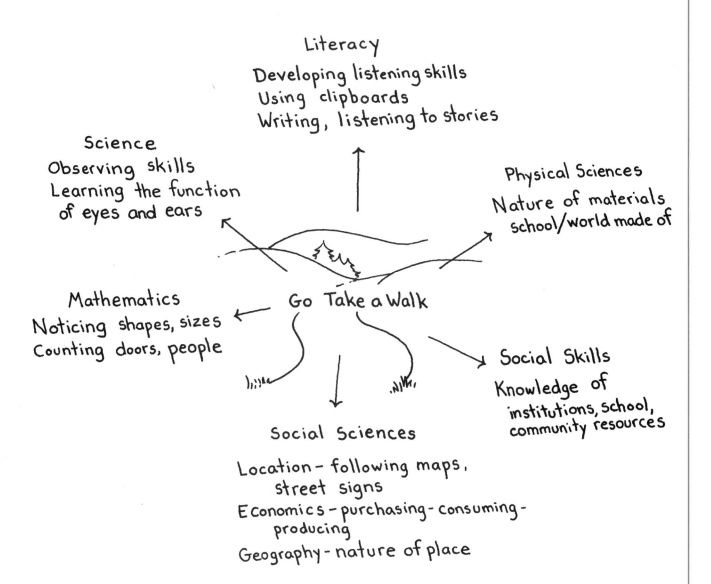

Literacy
Developing listening skills
Using clipboards
Writing, listening to stories

Science
Observing skills
Learning the function
of eyes and ears

Physical Sciences
Nature of materials
school/world made of

Go Take a Walk

Mathematics
Noticing shapes, sizes
Counting doors, people

Social Skills
Knowledge of
institutions, school,
community resources

Social Sciences

Location - following maps,
street signs
Economics - purchasing - consuming -
producing
Geography - nature of place

167

Playing to Learn on a Birthday

Today **Lisa** is **4**!

"Happy birthday to you, happy birthday to you," the children sing to one another, even though it's no one's birthday. There's something special about birthdays—the "Happy Birthday" song, the fun of celebrating one's life, and the joy of being special for one day. In quality schools, birthday celebrations that are integrated into the total curriculum are not only times for joyful celebrations, but for learning as well.

Because birthdays are of high interest to children, they hold a multitude of learning opportunities. When children of differing ethnic heritages are in the group, the whole world opens up to them as they experience the same holiday celebrated in different ways. Literature, myths, and songs are part of the celebration. Mathematics, music, early writing and reading, and many of the social sciences also can be integral parts of a birthday celebration.

Birthday celebrations are both appropriate and foster learning when they:
- ★ *are planned as integral parts of the day's routines*
- ★ *foster the goals of the program and curriculum*
- ★ *consider alternative views of the same holidays and beliefs*
- ★ *are appropriate for the age and maturity of the children*

Connecting Home and School
Before Beginning Birthday Celebrations

Before you begin celebrating birthdays, survey parents to find out how they celebrate birthdays. You can do this informally as families enroll their children, or more formally at a parent meeting devoted to curriculum and program planning. Ask parents how they expect you to celebrate children's birthdays. For example, some religions forbid birthday celebrations; therefore, you'll want to find out how families feel about celebrations. Ask:

- ★ How would you like your child's special day recognized?

- ★ Are there any special customs you would like to share with the other children?

After you find out the families' desires, you can plan wonderful birthday celebrations. This chapter offers many ideas for celebrating children's birthdays. You can use some for every birthday experience. However, you may or may not choose others on a given birthday. Fill the children's day with joy and learning by helping them:

★ *practice counting*

★ *participate in literacy experiences*

★ *learn about the scientific concepts of growth*

★ *enjoy traditional games and foods*

Mathematical Children

What better time to focus on mathematics than children's birthdays?

Think of all the opportunities to count, add, and subtract.

 **Birthday Crown**

Materials
Poster board
Markers and other decorations
Scissors
Tape

Make a birthday crown for the birthday child to wear.
If desired, make several crowns so the children can choose the one they want to wear on their birthday. (These should be relatively permanent because you'll use them all year.)
Along with the crowns, cut out the numerals 2 through 5 from a piece of poster board.
The children can use these to attach to the crown.
Ask the birthday child to select a crown along with the numeral representing his age.

Your Birthday Number

Materials
None needed

During the day, ask the birthday child to select the number of children, including himself, that equal his age. For example, if the child is five-years-old, ask him to select enough children (including himself) to equal five. These five children will:

★ take notices to the office

★ feed the pets and water the plants

★ play a game

★ work at a special table

Count the Days

Materials
Paper
Tape or glue

With the children, count the days before a birthday.
If you work with three-year-olds, you could make a paper chain consisting of four or five rings. Four or five days before a child's birthday, remove one of the rings. Count the remaining rings and say, "Now there are only three days left before it's your birthday."
Continue removing rings until it's the child's birthday.

Calendar Counting

Materials
Blank calendar, or large piece of poster board and markers

Encourage four- and five-year-olds to use a calendar to count the days before their birthday. Make a large calendar, leaving enough space for the children to draw or write the events that occur during a given day.
Mark all the birthdays and other special days with symbols to remind the children of the event.

Five-year-olds can:

★ count the days that have passed
since their birthday

★ count the days until the next child's birthday

Rather than having a routine morning activity,
use the calendar to introduce news and record
special events. When the month is over,
hang up the calendar.
Children will gravitate to the record
of their life in the classroom,
talking about and discussing events of the past.

SEPTEMBER

SUNDAY	MONDAY	TUESDAY	WEDNESDAY	THURSDAY	FRIDAY	SATURDAY
			1	2	3	5
4 yrs for Lisa! 6	7	8	9			
13	14	15	16			
			5 yrs for Tim!			
20	21	22	23			
	5 yrs. For Jenny!					
27	28	29	3			

Decorate the Cake

Materials

Heavy white paper
Scissors
Markers
Glue sticks
Sparkles
Chart paper

Before the school year begins, draw several "birthday cake" shapes
on heavy white paper and cut them out.
Keep a special set of markers, a glue stick, and some sparkles on reserve for the birthday child.
When a child has a birthday, glue one of the cakes onto a piece of chart paper
and write the child's name underneath it.
Encourage the birthday child to use the special materials to decorate his cake.
When he is done, ask him to draw the number of candles on the cake to equal his age.
During the day, refer to the birthday child's age. For example, say things such as,
"Yesterday you were three years old, now you're four, and next year you will be five."

173

Birthday Chart

Materials

Wrapping paper or any large sheet of paper

Tape

Markers

Make a birthday statistics chart with the birthday child.

Tape a large sheet of wrapping paper, a little longer than the child's height, to the wall.

Ask the birthday child to stand next to the paper and trace around his body.

Measure the child's height and weight.

In bold print, label the page with the child's full name, the date he was born,

the current date, the child's height, weight, and age.

Literate Children

There are many poems and birthday stories from which you can choose for a birthday celebration. Birthdays also offer many opportunities for children to express their ideas through symbols—whether they are scribbling, drawing, or using invented writing.

Growing Up

Materials

Poems about growing up, such as "The End," from *When We Were Very Young* by A. A. Milne

Paper, and crayons or markers

Stapler

Construction paper

A great poem to read to the children is "The End" in *When We Were Very Young,*

which is a poem about growing up.

The poem begins, "When I was one, I was just begun," and continues through age six.

After you read the poem, encourage the children to draw or write a page about when they were

one, two, three, four, or until their current age. Staple together the pages between two pieces of

construction paper to make a "Growing Book."

Or make a chart with the children, illustrating what they did

when they were one, two, three, and so on.

A Birthday Book

Materials
Paper
Crayons or markers
Stapler
Construction paper

Make a class book for the birthday child.
Ask each child to draw or write a page for the book, wishing the child a happy birthday.
Staple together the pages between two sheets of heavy construction paper. On the front cover,
write the child's name, the date, and title it "Happy Birthday!"
While the others are making the birthday child's book,
encourage the birthday child to dictate or write his own book.
Ask the birthday child to write about his favorite foods, things he likes to do, his friends, and
other things. Ask him to predict what he will learn during the coming year.
If your program is not year-round, make sure the children who will not receive a birthday book
get a different book from the class. For example, they can make a "Happy Day" book, a "Get
Well" book, or some other book to celebrate the child's life.

Books for Older Children

Materials
See suggestions below

For older children, read:
★ Bill Martin's *Knots on a Counting Rope,* the story of a Native American grandfather who tells his
son about growing up and growing older.
★ *A Birthday Basket for Tia* by Pat Mora, the story of a child preparing a birthday basket for her
beloved great aunt who will be 92. This book describes Mexican American birthday customs.
★ *Birthday Presents* by Cynthia Rylant, a joyous story about a child who is told about each of her
birthdays from her birth until age six.

Connecting Home and School

Make the home-school connection by asking families to continue the birthday custom of sharing special remembrances of their children's birthdays. The following is a sample letter that you could send to families.

Dear Families,

We have just read **Birthday Presents** by Cynthia Rylant. In this story, a family tells their little girl the story of what happened on each of her birthdays, beginning with the day of her birth.

It would be fun for your child to hear about your family history and memories on each of his or her birthdays. If you send in photographs or a few notes about special things that happened on your child's birthday, we can talk about them at school.

Thank you for your continuing support of our program.

Sincerely,

Birthday Cards

Materials
Paper, and crayons or markers
Envelopes and stamps

Making birthday cards offers another opportunity for literacy learning.
As a group, ask the children to write, draw, or dictate a birthday card for the birthday child.
This card doesn't have to be a secret, so you can involve the birthday child.
Address and stamp a large envelope, and then take a trip to the post office to mail it.
At the post office, encourage the children to look at different stamps,
find out how mail is sorted, and how the letter carriers find their homes.
When you return from the post office, ask each child to draw, write, or dictate a letter to himself.
Show three- and four-year-olds how to write an address on the envelope.
Five-year-olds may be able to print their address or dictate it to you.
Give the children an assortment of postage stamps and ask them to select
the stamp they want on their card.
The best part of the whole project is when the children receive their card in the mail!

Make Your Own Post Office

Materials
Rubber stamps, old receipt books, junk mail stamps, sorting trays, and so on
Empty shoeboxes
Tape, glue, or stapler
Marker

Set up a post office in the Dramatic Play Area. Equip the area with rubber stamps, old receipt
books, junk mail stamps, envelopes, sorting trays, and a cash register.
Continue post office play by making a mailbox for each child in the class.
(For example, make mailboxes by joining together
shoeboxes and labeling them with the children's names.)

Learning Letters

Materials
Chart paper
Pen
Rubber alphabet stamps and plastic or wooden letters
Paper
Markers
Index cards

Use the meaning of the day to introduce phoneme awareness. You might:

★ Write the birthday child's name on a chart. As you do so, identify each letter.

★ Write all the children's names on a chart. Ask them to look at the chart and find a name that begins with the same letter as the birthday child's name.

★ Suggest that four- and five-year-olds look around the classroom for letters that are the same as the initial and ending letters of their own name.

★ Create a Writing Center. In the center, include rubber alphabet block stamps, plastic letters, paper, and markers. Print the children's names on index cards. Encourage each child to use his card as a model to assemble his name with plastic letters or to print his name.

Growing Children

Birthdays are good times to introduce the concept of growth, change, and the continuity of life.
Some children think that on their birthday, everything will change on that day and
they'll be bigger and taller. And, because they are older, they will be able to do
all the things people tell them they can do "when they grow up and are older."

Talk About Growing

Materials
Books about growing (suggestions listed below)

To start a discussion about the slowness and continuity of growing, you might read the children:
★ *Happy Birthday, Sam* by Pat Hutchins, the story of a boy who finds he is still too short
to reach many things, even though he's a year older.
★ *Titch* by Pat Hutchins, the story of a boy who is jealous of his older brother
and sister because everything they get is bigger than the things he gets.
★ *You'll Soon Grow Into Them, Titch* by Pat Hutchins, the story of a boy who outgrows his own
clothes only to find that the hand-me-downs he's given are too big.
★ *Growing-Up Feet* by Beverly Cleary, the story of twins whose feet haven't grown up enough for
new shoes, so they settle for bright red boots instead. Take a survey of the shoes the children are
wearing. How many are wearing boots? Tie-shoes? Red or blue shoes?

Guess Who?

Materials
Photographs of the children as babies
Poster board
Tape
Markers

Ask the families to send in a photo of their child, as well as themselves,
when their child was a baby.
Tape the photos to a piece of poster board. Title it "Guess Who?"
Do not label the pictures—number them instead.
Children will enjoy finding their own picture and those of their friends.

Now ask the teachers, administrators, building engineers, cafeteria workers,
and custodians to bring in a picture of when they were babies.
Tape these photos on a poster board and identify them by number, not names.
Watch as adults and children alike try to guess who is who. Make a list with the number of each
photograph and the person's name. Attach a folder to the bottom of the board
and put the list with the names into it.
Talk about the changes that occur when one grows. Remind the children that
they'll always be the same person even though they grow and are older.

Birthdays in the Past

Materials
Cake
Numeral candles

Ask an elder volunteer or perhaps one of the children's relatives
to share their birthday with the children.
Bring in a cake for the volunteer, along with candles in the shape of numerals.
Encourage the children to say the name of the numeral (50, 60, 70, or whatever it is).
Ask the children if they can clap that many times.
After you enjoy the cake, the volunteer can tell the children about:
★ what they did on their birthday when they were the children's ages
★ what they enjoy doing now that they are older
★ how birthday celebrations have changed over the years

"Happy birthday, happy birthday, happy birthday to you," the children sing as they play in the sand, run in the play yard, or sit by themselves and sing to a doll. Children sing the birthday song whether or not there's a birthday taking place. Perhaps the children love the song so much because it's familiar. In fact, it was written just for them by Patty Smith Hill in the late 1800s as a part of the first kindergarten curriculum. Whatever the reason, a birthday celebration begins and ends with singing, "Happy Birthday."

Songs and Music

Materials
None needed

After you've sung "Happy Birthday," there's time for other songs and music.
Because birthdays are days for children to feel really loved,
they're also good days to sing songs of love.
While children are working and playing, you could begin singing the song:

Love somebody, yes I do!
Love somebody, yes I do.
Love somebody, yes I do.
Love somebody but I won't say who.

As you sing, enjoy the smiles of the children who smile at you,
because they know that you're singing about them!
If possible, obtain a copy of "A You're Adorable," the 1940s love song that begins:

A you're adorable,
B you're so beautiful...

The song continues through the entire alphabet.
Sing:

I love you, you love me, we're a happy family.
With a knick, knack, paddy whack, give the dog a bone,
All our love comes rolling home.

Marching Birthday Band

Materials
Rhythm band instruments
March music

A birthday celebration calls for a marching band.
Of course, the leader of the band will be the birthday child.
Play a march on the piano or play a CD of children's favorite marches.
You might select "This Land Is Your Land," a John Phillip Sousa march, "Stars and Stripes
Forever," or make up a song to "When the Saints Go Marching In," changing the words to
"When the Children Go Marching In."

Mathematical Marching

Materials
Rhythm band instruments

Integrate mathematical ideas into the marching band
by asking the children to select instruments to play.
For example, you may have four drums. Say, "We have four drums. Who wants to start by playing a drum?"
Choose one child to play a drum, and ask that child to choose the number
of children needed to play the remaining drums.
Remind the children that there are a total of four drums and Carmen has one of them. Ask,
"How many more children should Carmen pick to be drummers?"
Continue the selection with rhythm sticks, tambourines, triangles, and so on until all the children
have an instrument. Try to use a different number of each type of instrument,
such as six tambourines, three triangles, and so on.
Ask the children to think about which instruments they want to begin playing as they march,
reminding them that everyone will have a turn with the instruments they want to play.
March around the room a couple of times to the first march.
Then, ask the birthday child to choose a new leader. Ask the children to exchange instruments
and march again until everyone has had a turn with the instruments
of their choice or when everyone needs to stop and rest.

Time to Rest

Materials
Parade by Donald Crews

When you've finished marching and need to rest, gather the children on the story rug
and read *Parade* by Donald Crews.
This book is about all the elements of a parade, including the spectators,
street vendors, marchers, bands, floats, and cleanup.
You may want to plan for more of these elements the next time you have a marching band.

Birthday Fun and Games

Birthdays are great times to play traditional birthday party games and enjoy party food!

I Made Ice Cream!

Materials
Ingredients to make ice cream (see recipe below)
Poster board and marker
Measuring cups and spoons
Timer

Copy the ice cream recipe (see next page) onto a piece of poster board.
Read the recipe with the children, showing them the steps involved.
Ask them to think about whether they want vanilla or chocolate ice cream
and vote for the flavor they want.
Each child will get to choose his favorite flavor, but record the votes to determine which flavor is
the most popular.

Ice Cream
¼ cup (60 ml) milk, half-and-half, or heavy cream
1-2 drops of vanilla extract or ½ teaspoon (2 ml) chocolate syrup
1 teaspoon (7 g) sugar
1 cup of ice
½ cup (125 g) salt
Small and medium size zipper-closure plastic bags

Working with a volunteer, help each child measure and pour one teaspoon of sugar,
¼ cup milk or cream, and one or two drops of vanilla or ½ teaspoon of chocolate syrup
into a small zipper-closure baggie.
Carefully seal the bag.
Ask the children to shake the bag to mix the ingredients a bit.
Then, give each child a larger zipper-closure baggie. Help them measure a cup of ice and ½ cup of
salt (to lower the temperature of the ice) and pour it into the baggie.
Place the smaller baggie with the milk mixture into the larger baggie
with the ice and salt. Make sure this bag is also securely sealed.
Set a timer for five minutes. Encourage the children to shake their baggies until ice cream forms.
Eat the ice cream right away, or label each bag with the children's names
and place them in the freezer for a treat later in the day.

What Did We Learn?

Materials
None needed

Reflect on the ice cream-making experience.
Ask the children what they liked best about making and eating the ice cream.
Ask them why they think they needed salt to make the ice cream.

Books About Ice Cream

Materials
Books about making or eating ice cream, such as:
★ *Curious George Goes to an Ice Cream Shop* by Margaret Rey
★ *From Cow to Ice Cream* by Bertram Knight

Read Margaret Rey's *Curious George Goes to an Ice Cream Shop* and ask the children what flavors
they would choose when they make ice cream again.
Although children made ice cream in baggies, ask them if they know where ice cream comes from.
Read Bertram Knight's *From Cow to Ice Cream*.
Because this book is for older children, you may need to "read" the pictures
and summarize the text for younger children.

Party Games

Materials

See suggestions below

Keep a few party games on hand for birthdays (for example, Ten-Pins,
Pin the Tail on the Donkey, Grand Mufti, and Hide and Go Seek).

★ Ten-Pins—Make ten-pins from discarded soda bottles. Fill the bottles with sand
and cover them securely. Place as many pins as the child is old and ask the children to take turns
knocking them down by rolling a ball toward them.

★ Pin the Tail on the Donkey—Draw a large donkey on a piece of poster board
and cut out a couple of tails, or purchase a game. Use a strip of lightweight tissue or crepe paper
to cover the children's eyes. (Discard this piece after each child wears it for sanitation.)
Put two-sided tape on the tails instead of pins. Three-year-olds can stand just a foot or two away
from the donkey and walk toward it. Four-year-olds can stand a bit further away from the donkey,
and five-year-olds can turn around a couple of times after they are blindfolded
and then try to put the tail on the donkey.

★ Grand Mufti—The birthday child gets to be the leader ("Grand Mufti") when playing this
game. Ask the children to hold hands and form a circle. The birthday child
stands in the middle of the circle and says, "The Grand Mufti says …" and gives a command.
For example, "The Grand Mufti says, 'Stand on one foot, …jump, …turn around,' " and so on.
When the Mufti gives a command without saying, "The Grand Mufti says…," the children do not
do the command. The birthday child can choose others to be the Grand Mufti, if desired.

★ Hide & Seek—Read *Hide & Seek* by Rosella Badessa, the story of animals playing traditional
playground games. Encourage the children to select some of these games to play,
just like their parents or grandparents did.

replace
the cap…

seal the
lid with
tape…

Happy
4th
Birthday!

write a birthday
message and
cover the bottle!

185

What Did You Do Learn on a Birthday?

Assessing and Evaluating

What Did the Children Learn?

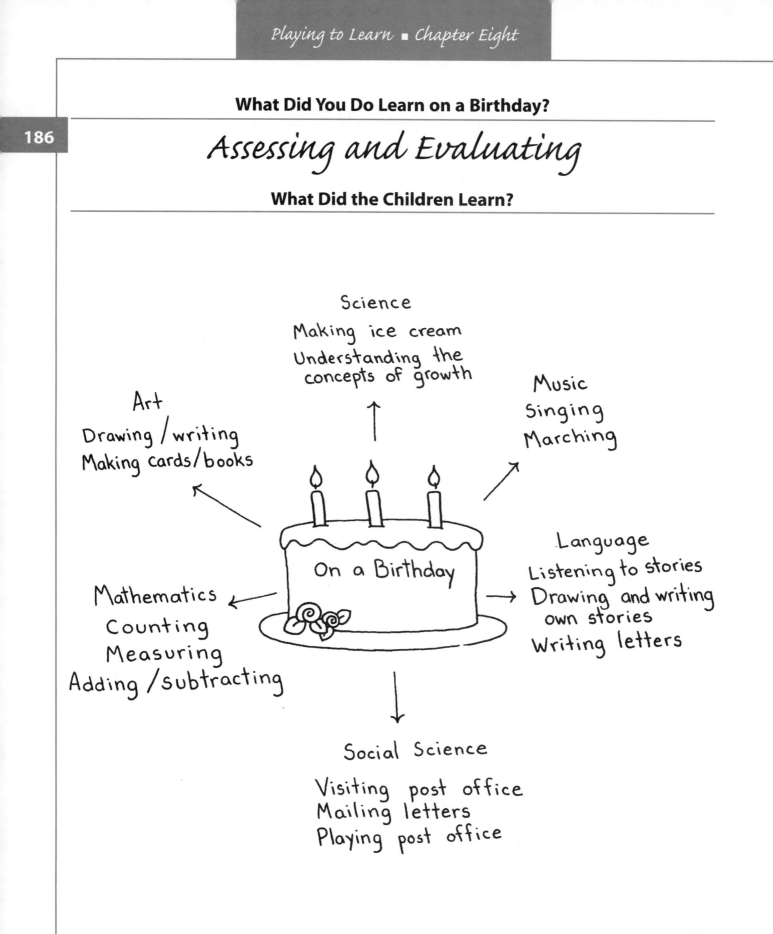

Science
Making ice cream
Understanding the
concepts of growth

Music
Singing
Marching

Art
Drawing / writing
Making cards / books

On a Birthday

Language
Listening to stories
Drawing and writing
own stories
Writing letters

Mathematics
Counting
Measuring
Adding / subtracting

Social Science
Visiting post office
Mailing letters
Playing post office

Books for Children

Ada, A.F. (1997). *Gathering the sun: An alphabet in Spanish and English.* New York: Lothrop, Lee & Shepherd.

Archambault, J., Endicott, J., & B. Martin. (1988). *Listen to the rain.* New York: Holt, Rinehart & Company.

Asbjornsen, P.C. & J.E. Moe. (1970). *East o' the sun and west o' the moon: Fifty-nine Norwegian folk tales.* New York: Dover Publishers.

Badessa, R. (1999). *Hide & seek (Let's play ser).* London: Child's Play International Ltd.

Ballard, R. (1994). *Good-bye, house.* New York: Greenwillow.

Belafonte, H. (1999). *Island in the sun.* New York: Dial Books.

Berenstain, S. & J. Berenstain. (1987). *The berenstain bears and the trouble with friends.* New York: Random House.

Branley, F.M. & J.G. Hale. (1997). *Down comes the rain.* New York: Harper Collins.

Bursill, H. (1997). *Hand shadows and more hand shadows: A series of novel and amusing figures formed by the hand.* New York: Dover Press.

Challoner, J. (1996). *Wet and dry.* New York: Raintree.

Chappell, J.A. (1991). *Little johnny raindrop.* New York: State House Press.

Ciardi, J. (1987). *You read to me, I'll read to you.* New York: Harper.

Cleary, B. (1987). *Growing-up feet.* New York: William Morrow & Company.

Climo, S. (1995). *The little red ant and the great big crumb: A Mexican fable.* New York: Clarion Books.

Cohen, M. (1989). *Will I have a friend?* New York: Aladdin Paperbacks.

Crews, D. (1986). *Parade.* New York: Mulberry Books.

Danis, N. (1995). *Walk with me.* New York: Cartwheel Books.

De Coteau Orie, S. (1996). *Did you hear the wind sing your name?* New York: Walker & Company.

Degen, B. (1995). *Jamberry*. New York: Harperfestival.

Demi. (1999). *Kites: Magic wishes that fly up to the sky*. New York: Crown Publishers.

Dorros, A. (1990). *Feel the wind*. New York: Harper Trophy.

Dotich, R.K. (1998). *Lemonade sun: And other summer poems*. New York: Boyds Mills Press.

Eastman, P.D. (1990). *Perro grande...perro pequeno*. New York: Random House Español.

Eberts, M. (1984). *Pancakes, crackers and pizza: A book about shapes*. New York: Children's Press.

Elliott, D. (1984). *Alligators and music*. Cambridge: Harvard Common Press.

English, K. (1996). *Big wind coming!* New York: Albert Williams & Co.

Ets, M.H. (1978). *Gilberto and the wind*. New York: Viking Press.

Evans, L. (1995). *Rain song*. New York: Houghton Mifflin Company.

Field, E. (1996). *Poems of childhood*. New York: Atheneum.

Gershator, P. (1998). *Greetings, sun*. New York: DK Publishing.

Gibbons, G. (1995). *Catch the wind!: All about kites*. New York: Little, Brown & Co.

Ginsburg, M. (1997). *Mushroom in the rain*. New York: Aladdin Paperbacks.

Giovanni, N. (1996). *The sun is so quiet: Poems*. New York: Henry Holt & Co.

Hallinan, P.K. (2000). *My first day of school*. New York: Hambleton-Hill Publishing.

Hesse, K. (1999). *Come on, rain!* New York: Scholastic Trade.

Heo, Y. (1994). *One afternoon*. New York: Orchard Books.

Hoban, T. (1996). *Shapes, shapes, shapes*. New York: Mulberry Books.

Hoberman, M.A. (1998). *Miss mary mack: A hand-clapping rhyme*. New York: Little, Brown & Co.

Hughes, L. (1995). "April rain song." In A. Rampersad & D. Roessel (Eds.), *The collected poems of Langston Hughes*. New York: Vintage.

Hughes, L. (1995). "Garment." In A. Rampersad & D. Roessel (Eds.), *The collected poems of Langston Hughes*. New York: Vintage.

Hughes, S. (1999). *Let's join in*. Cambridge, MA: Candlewick Press.

Hutchins, P. (1993). *Titch*. New York: Aladdin Paperbacks.

Hutchins, P. (1993). *The wind blew*. New York: Aladdin Paperbacks.

Hutchins, P. (1999). *Happy birthday, Sam*. New York: Econo-Clad Books.

Hutchins, P. (1999). *You'll soon grow into them, Titch.* New York: Econo-Clad Books.

Jenkins, S. (1996). *Big & little.* New York: Houghton Mifflin Co.

Knight, B.T. (1997). *From cow to ice cream.* New York: Children's Press.

Knowlton, L.L. (1995). *Why cowboys sleep with their boots on.* New York: Pelican Publishing Co.

Komaiko, L. (2000). *Annie bananie.* New York: Econo-Clad Books.

Lear, E. (1999). *A book of nonsense.* Ware, Hertfordshire: Wordsworth Editions Ltm.

London, J. (1999). *Puddles.* UK: Puffin Books.

Martin, B & J. Archambault. (1987). *Knots on a counting rope.* New York: Henry Holt & Co.

Marzollo, J. (1995). *Sun song.* New York: Harper Collins.

McDermott, G. (1974). *Arrow to the sun: A Pueblo Indian tale.* New York: Viking Press.

McQuade, J. (1999). *At preschool with teddy bear.* New York: Dial Books.

Milne, A.A. (1988). "Rice pudding." In *When we were very young.* New York: E.P. Dutton.

Milne, A.A. (1988). "The king's breakfast." In *When we were very young.* New York: E.P. Dutton.

Milne, A.A. (1992). "The End." In *Now we are six.* UK: Puffin Books.

Mitra, A. (1998). *Chloe's sunny day.* New York: Sterling Publications.

Mora, P. (1992). *A birthday basket for Tia.* New York: Simon & Schuster.

Morris, A. (1993). *Hats, hats, hats.* New York: Mulberry Press.

Olivero, J. (1995). *The day sun was stolen.* New York: Hyperion.

Otten, C. (1997). *January rides the wind: A book of poems for children.* New York: Lothrop, Lee & Shepard.

Poulsson, E. (1979). *Finger plays for nursery and kindergarten.* New York: Dover Press.

Prelutsky, J. (2000). *It's raining pigs and noodles.* New York: Greenwillow.

Raffi. (1990). *One light, one sun (Raffi songs to read).* New York: Crown Publishers.

Rey, M. (1977). *Curious george flies a kite.* New York: Houghton Mifflin Co.

Rey, M. (1989). *Curious george and the ice cream store.* New York: Houghton Mifflin Co.

Roche, H. (1998). *Pete's puddles.* New York: Houghton Mifflin Co.

Rockwell, A.F. (1989). *Apples and pumpkins.* New York: Simon and Schuster.

Russo, M. (2000). *The Big Brown Box.* New York: Greenwillow.

Rylant, C. (1991). *Birthday presents*. New York: Orchard Books.

Shaw, C. (1988). *It looked like spilt milk*. New York: Harper Collins.

Silverstein, S. (1974). *Where the sidewalk ends*. New York: Harper Collins.

Small, D. (2000). *Imogene's antlers*. New York: Crown Publishers.

Stevenson, R.L. (1999). *My shadow*. Cambridge, MA: Candlewick Press.

Turner, B.C. (1998). *Flutes (The musical instruments of the world)*. Smart Apple Media.

Udry, J.M. (1988). *Let's be enemies*. New York: Harper Trophy.

Weiss, L. (1999). *My teacher sleeps at school*. New York: Econo-Clad Books.

Yee, W.H. (1995). *Drop of rain*. New York: Houghton Mifflin Co.

Yolen, J. (1988). *The emperor and the kite*. New York: Putnam Publishing Group.

Books and Articles for Teachers

Bredekamp, S. & T. Rosegrant. (1995). *Reaching potentials: Transforming early childhood curriculum and assessment* (Volume II). Washington, DC: National Association for the Education of Young Children (NAEYC).

Bredekamp, S. & C. Copple. (1997). *Developmentally appropriate practice in early childhood programs* (rev. ed.). Washington, DC: National Association for the Education of Young Children (NAEYC).

Dewey, J. (1944). *Democracy and education*. New York: The Free Press.

Dighee, J., Z. Calomiris & C. Van Zupthen. (1998). Nurturing the language of art in children. *Young Children, 53*(1), 4-9.

Hazen, N., B. Black, & F. Fleming-Johnson. (1984). Social acceptance: Strategies children use and how teachers can help children learn. *Young Children, 39*(6), 70-75.

Johnson, B. (1998). *Cup cooking*. Lake Alfred, FL: Early Educators Press.

Piaget, J. & B. Inhelder. (1969). *The psychology of the child*. New York: Basic Books.

Seefeldt, C. (1993). Learning for freedom. *Young Children, 48*(3), 4-13.

Seefeldt, C. (1995). Art: A serious work. *Young Children, 50*(3), 39-54.

Seefeldt, C. & A. Galper. (1998). *Continuing issues in early childhood education* (2nd ed.). Upper Saddle River, NJ: Prentice-Hall/Merrill.

Seefeldt, C. & A.Galper. (2001). *Active experiences for active children: Language arts*. Upper Saddle River, NJ: Prentice-Hall/Merrill.

Vygotsky, L. (1986). *Thought and language*. Cambridge, MA: MIT Press.

2-year-olds
age appropriateness, 11–12
circle games, 100–101
fine motor play, 89–90
large motor play, 87–88
skill games, 101
wet and dry, 60

3-year-olds
age appropriateness, 11–12
circle games, 102–104
fine motor play, 89–90
gardening activities, 51
large motor play, 87–88
skill games, 101
writing skills, 177

4-year-olds
age appropriateness, 11–12
books for, 175
chasing games, 105
circle games, 102–105
counting, 172
fine motor play, 91, 95–97
gardening activities, 50–51
large motor play, 90
multicultural books, 76
reading skills, 178
riddles, 118
science activities, 91–93
skill games, 105–107
time capsules, 50
writing skills, 177

5-year-olds
age appropriateness, 11–12
books for, 175
chasing games, 105
circle games, 103–105
counting, 172–173
fine motor play, 91, 95–97
gardening activities, 50–51
large motor play, 90
multicultural books, 76
reading skills, 178
riddles, 118
science activities, 91–93
skill games, 105–106
weather predicting, 71–72
writing skills, 177

A
Age appropriateness, 9, 11
Aggressive children, 143–144
Alarm clocks, 91
Aluminum foil, 30
Ant farms, 141
Apples, 166
Appliances, 91
boxes, 39
Aquariums, 141
Art materials, 19, 30, 46, 52, 147
Art activities
birthday, 173, 177
hot and sunny day, 51–52
perfectly beautiful day, 96–97
wet and rainy day, 35
when taking a walk, 152
when you have to wait, 135–136
windy day, 71, 73, 81
Assessment, 14
birthday activities, 186
hot and sunny day activities, 64
perfectly beautiful day activities, 108
wet and rainy day activities, 41
when taking a walk, 167
when things go wrong, 148
when you have to wait, 128
windy day activities, 83
Association for Childhood Education
International, 10
Autoharps, 24

B
Backpacks, 98
Bags, 96, 119, 124
decorated, 111–112
paper, 79
zippered plastic, 79, 183
Baking pans, 62, 92, 100
Balance builders, 22, 106
Balloons, 24
Balls, 101, 105–106, 126, 185
Ping-Pong, 67
Bamboo poles, 51
Basketball, 105
Baskets, 105, 126
Beanbags, 101
Beans, 158
Beginning of school, 132–134

Bicycles, 60, 88
Binder clips, 32
Birthday celebrations, 169–186
Blankets, 39, 51, 95
Blenders, 156
Blocks, 89, 106
hollow, 26, 39, 99–100
parquetry, 124
plastic, 30
unit, 117
wooden, 30
Bolts, 91
Books, 12, 141, 163
about animals, 151, 157
about ice cream, 184
Alligators and Music by Donald
Elliott, 82, 188
Annie Bananie by Leah Komaiko,
135, 189
Apples and Pumpkins by Ann F.
Rockwell, 166, 189
*Arrow to the Sun: A Pueblo Indian
Tale* by Gerald McDermott, 63,
189
At Preschool With Teddy Bear by
Jacqueline McQuade, 131, 189
Beast Feast: Poems by Douglas
Florian, 107
*The Berenstain Bears and the Trouble
With Friends* by Stan & Jan
Berenstain, 138, 187
Big & Little by Steve Jenkins, 118,
189
The Big Brown Box by Marisabina
Russo, 95, 190
Big Wind Coming! by Karen
English, 80, 188
A Birthday Basket for Tia by Pat
Mora, 175, 189
Birthday Presents by Cynthia Rylant,
175–176, 190
birthday, 175
A Book of Nonsense by Edward Lear,
189
Catch the Wind! All About Kites by
Gail Gibbons, 75, 188
Chloe's Sunny Day by Annie Mitra,
45, 189
The Cloud Book by Tomie dePaola,
70

Collected Poems by Langston Hughes, 36, 111, 188

Come On, Rain! by Karen Hesse, 36, 188

Curious George and the Ice Cream Store by Margret Rey, 184, 189

Curious George Flies a Kite by Margret Rey, 76, 189

The Day Sun Was Stolen by Jamie Olivero, 63, 189

Did You Hear the Wind Sing Your Name? by Sandra De Coteau Orie, 81, 187

Down Comes the Rain by F. M. Branley & J. G. Hale, 187

A Drop of Rain by Wong Herbert Yee, 37, 190

East o' the Sun and West o' the Moon: Fifty-Nine Norwegian Folk Tales by Peter Christen Asbjornsen & J.E. Moe, 63, 187

An Edward Lear Alphabet by Edward Lear, 111–112

The Emperor and the Kite by Jane Yolen, 76, 190

Feel the Wind by Arthur Dorros, 80, 188

Finger Plays for Nursery and Kindergarten by Emilie Poulsson, 107, 189

Flutes by Barry Carson Turner, 82, 190

folk tales, 63

for children, 187–190

for older children, 175

for teachers, 190

friends, 135

From Cow to Ice Cream by Bertram Knight, 184, 189

Gathering the Sun: An Alphabet in Spanish and English by Alma Flor Ada, 63, 187

Gilberto and the Wind by Marie Hall Ets, 73, 188

Good-Bye, House by Robin Ballard, 136, 187

Greetings, Sun by Phyllis Gershator, 45, 188

Growing-Up Feet by Beverly Cleary, 179, 187

Hand Shadows and More Hand Shadows by Henry Bursill, 54, 187

Happy Birthday, Sam by Pat Hutchins, 179, 189

Hats, Hats, Hats by Ann Morris, 51, 189

Hide & Seek by Rosella Badessa, 185, 187

Higgle Wiggle: Happy Rhymes by Eve Merriam, 107

Imogene's Antlers by David Small, 125, 190

Island in the Sun by Harry Belafonte, 63, 187

It Looked Like Spilt Milk by Charles G. Shaw, 71, 190

It's Raining Pigs & Noodles: Poems by Jack Prelutsky, 116, 189

Jamberry by Bruce Degen, 125, 188

January Rides the Wind by Charlotte Otten, 67, 189

Kites: Magic Wishes That Fly Up to the Sky by Demi, 76, 188

Knots on a Counting Rope by Bill Martin, Jr. & John Archambault, 175, 189

Lemonade Sun: And Other Summer Poems by Rebecca Kai Dotich, 49, 188

Let's Be Enemies by Janice Udry, 138, 190

Let's Join In by Shirley Hughes, 107, 188

Listen to the Rain by John Archambault, James Endicott & Bill Martin, Jr., 39, 187

Little Johnny Raindrop by James Chappell, 30, 187

The Little Red Ant and the Great Big Crumb: A Mexican Fable by Shirley Climo, 118, 187

making, 13, 38, 68, 71, 135–136, 151, 175

measurement, 118

Miss Mary Mack: A Hand-Clapping Rhyme by Mary Ann Hoberman, 125, 188

Mother Goose, 113

Mushroom in the Rain by Mirra Ginsburg, 35, 39, 188

My First Day of School by P.K. Hallinan, 131, 188

My Shadow by Robert Louis Stevenson, 53, 190

My Teacher Sleeps in School by Leatie Weiss, 163, 190

One Afternoon by Yumi Heo, 160, 188

One Light, One Sun by Raffi, 63, 189

Pancakes, Crackers and Pizza: A Book About Shapes by Marjorie Eberts, 124, 188

Parade by Donald Crews, 183, 187

Perro Grande . . . Perro Pequeno by P.D. Eastman, 118, 188

Pete's Puddles by Hannah Roche, 33, 189

Poems of Childhood by E. Field, 123, 188

poetry, 63, 67, 107, 111–116, 123

Puddles by Jonathon London, 33, 189

Rain Song by Lezlie Evans, 24, 37, 188

rainy day, 38

saying good-bye, 134–136

Shapes, Shapes, Shapes by Tana Hoban, 124, 188

silly, 125–127

social skills, 138

The Sun Is So Quiet: Poems by Nikki Giovanni, 63, 188

Sun Song by Jean Marzollo, 63, 189

Titch by Pat Hutchins, 179, 188

Walk With Me by Naomi Danis, 159, 187

Wet and Dry by Jack Challoner, 60, 187

When We Were Very Young by A. A. Milne, 114, 174, 189

Where the Sidewalk Ends by Shel Silverstein, 116, 190

Why Cowboys Sleep With Their Boots On by Laurie Lazzaro Knowlton, 113, 189

Will I Have a Friend? by Miriam Cohen, 131, 187

The Wind Blew by Pat Hutchins, 68, 188

You Read to Me, I'll Read to You by John Ciardi, 115, 187

You'll Soon Grow into Them, Titch by Pat Hutchins, 179, 189

Bookshelves, 142

Bottles
pill, 158
soda, 185
squirt, 59–60, 92, 97

Bowls, 89

Box lids, 34

Boxes, 53, 89, 99, 101, 119, 124
appliance, 39, 87
cardboard, 39, 87, 95
grocery, 90
junk, 96
oatmeal, 88
plastic, 88–89, 93
shoe, 99, 177
tissue, 89
wood, 100

Bracelets, 90
Bread pans, 62
Bredekamp, S., 9–10, 190
Briefcases, 99
British Infant Schools, 46
Bubble mix, 58, 79
Bubble wands, 58, 79
Bubble wrap, 96
Buckets, 28, 35, 56–57, 60–61, 89, 92, 95–97
  paint, 61
Building toys, 91
Butter, 114
Buttons, 117

C
Cake, 180
Calendars, 172
Calomiris, Z., 190
Cameras, 23, 27, 69, 100, 133–134
Candles, 180
Cans, 35
Cardboard, 68
  buckets, 61
Cassette recorders, 141, 160
Catalogs, 99
CD players, 182
CDs, 182
Cereal, 142
Chairs, 51
  rocking, 141
Chalk, 53, 56, 59, 97, 106
Chart paper, 45, 48, 62, 69, 79, 92, 111, 114, 117, 119, 147, 173, 178
Chocolate
  frosty milk recipe, 49
  instant drink mix, 49
  syrup, 183
Circle games
  2-year-olds, 100–101
  3-year-olds, 102–104
  4-year-olds, 102–105
  5-year-olds, 103–105
Clay, 19, 56, 96
Clipboards, 12, 31, 33, 46, 54–55, 68, 71, 73–74, 153–154, 156, 158
Clothes
  damp, 32
  doll, 30
  dress-up, 100
  hangers, 38
  rainy day, 31–32
Clothesline, 32, 51, 60
Coffee pots, 92
Coffee, 55
Construction hats, 99
Construction paper, 13, 23, 30, 71, 73, 86, 94–97, 135–136, 151, 175

Containers, 28, 30–31, 34, 52, 57–59, 96
Cookie cutters, 92
Coolers, 46
Cooperation-building activities
  hot and sunny day, 58
  perfectly beautiful day, 98–100, 102–104
  wet and rainy day, 25, 37
  when you have to wait, 120, 126–127
  windy day, 75
Copple, C., 9
Copy machines, 156
Cots, 141
Counting activities, 172–173
Cowboy hats, 99
Crackers, 114, 142
Crayons, 33, 35–36, 46, 48–49, 55–57, 68, 73, 135–136, 152, 157, 175, 177
Credit cards, 98–99
Crepe paper, 185
Cupcake pans. *See* Muffin tins
Cupcake papers, 96
Cups, 142
  measuring, 47–49, 57, 92, 183
  paper, 46–49
  plastic, 54
Curtains, 100
Cutting boards, 166

D
Dewey, J., 9–10, 190
Dighee, J., 153, 190
Dirt. *See* Soil
Discipline, 140–144
Dishwashing liquid, 58, 60, 97
Doll clothes, 30
Dolls, 141–142
Dowels, 51
Dramatic play, 86, 98–100, 177
Drums, 17, 24, 127, 182
Duck, Duck, Goose, 104, 137
Duct tape, 96

E
Egg beaters, 59, 92, 156
Electrical tape, 22
Email, 136
Envelopes, 177
Exploratory play, 86–93
Eyedroppers, 30–31, 56

F
Fabric
  calico, 123
  gingham, 123

lightweight, 72
  loops, 25–26
  plaid, 111
  scraps, 52, 55, 96
  slick yellow, 99
  velvet, 100
  waterproof, 31–32
Facial tissue, 68
  boxes, 89
Fans, 67
Fasteners, 52
Fax machines, 156
Feathers, 52, 67, 96
Fertilizer, 165
Field trips, 99, 153, 161–166
  planning, 162
Film canisters, 158
Film, 23, 27, 69, 133–134
Fine motor skills
  hot and sunny day activities, 51–52, 54, 57, 61
  perfectly beautiful day activities, 89–93, 96
  preschooler activities, 91, 95–97
  toddler activities, 89–90
  wet and rainy day activity, 38
  windy day activities, 75–77
Fingerpaint, 97
Fingerplays, 121–123
Firefighter hats, 99
Fish, 141
  plastic, 61
Fishnets, 61
Flags, 80, 137
Flashlights, 98
Floor polishers, 156, 159
Flowers
  artificial, 96
  petals, 152
Funnels, 58, 88, 92, 185

G
Galper, A., 14, 73, 160
Garden hose, 58, 60–61, 98–100
Gardening activities, 50–51
Gardening flats, 99
Glue, 23, 52, 96, 132, 134, 138, 172, 177
  sticks, 173
Grand Mufti, 185
Graphing activities
  birthday, 174
  hot and sunny day, 57
  wet and rainy day, 28, 31
  when you have to wait, 114–115, 119–120
  windy day, 68–69, 79

Gravel, 55
Growth and development, 179–180
Guitars, 25

H
Half-and-half, 183
Handkerchief, 103
Hats, 51, 100
  birthday crowns, 171
  homemade, 51–52
  work, 99
Heavy cream, 183
Hide and Seek, 105, 185
Hill, Patty Smith, 181
Hole punches, 13, 38, 52, 72, 96
Hollow blocks, 26, 39, 99–100
Home-school connections, 19–20, 23,
  27–29, 32, 34, 38, 50, 116, 131,
  134, 147, 170, 176
Hourglasses, 125, 141
Housekeeping props, 100
Hula hoops, 25–26

I
I Spy, 123
Ice cream, 183–184
Ice
  blocks, 55
  chips, 48–49
  crushed, 183
  cubes, 47–49
Index cards, 112, 178
Inhelder, B., 9–10, 190
Insects, 92
Instant chocolate mix, 49
Instant coffee, 55
Invented spelling, 13–14

J
Jars, 125
  plastic, 54
Johnson, B., 190
Joining material, 91, 95
Juice, 142
  jugs, 55
Juicers, 48
Jump the Brook, 106
Junk boxes, 96
Junk mail, 177

K
Kiddie cars, 88
Kitchen timers, 125, 157, 183
Kitchen tools, 92
Kites, 75–76
Knives, 166

L
Language-building activities
  hot and sunny day, 62–63
  perfectly beautiful day, 93, 98–100,
    107
  wet and rainy day, 36–38
  when you take a walk, 153
  windy day, 67–68, 70–71, 81
Large motor skills
  hot and sunny day activities, 59–60
  perfectly beautiful day activities,
    87–88, 90, 105–106
  preschoolers, 90
  toddlers, 87–88
  wet and rainy day activities, 17–26
  when you have to wait, 126–127
  when you take a walk, 151–167
  windy day activities, 75, 78–79
Leaves, 61, 80, 92, 117, 152
Lemon juice, 47–48
Lemonade, 47–48
Lemons, 48
Letters
  plastic, 61, 111, 178
  rubber stamps, 178
  to authorities, 147
  to parents, 20, 29, 176
  wooden, 111, 178
Library cards, 163
Lights, 54
  flashlights, 98
Listening skill activities
  hot and sunny day, 62–63
  wet and rainy day, 36–38
  when you take a walk, 157–160
  windy day, 67–68, 73, 80–82
Literacy-building activities, 12–13
  birthday, 174–179, 183–185
  hot and sunny day, 45, 49, 51,
    53–54, 60, 63
  perfectly beautiful day, 95, 107
  wet and rainy day, 24, 30, 33,
    35–39
  when things go wrong, 131,
    134–136, 138, 141
  when you have to wait, 110–116,
    118, 123–127
  when you take a walk, 151, 157,
    159–160, 163, 166
  windy day, 67–68, 70–71, 73,
    75–76, 80–82
Lunch boxes, 99

M
Machines, 156, 159
Magnifying glasses, 92, 152
Maps, 98, 154, 164
  making, 161

Marbles, 125
Markers, 19, 23, 31, 33, 36–38, 46,
  48–49, 54–57, 61–62, 68–69,
  71–75, 79, 92, 111, 114, 117, 119,
  125, 132, 134-135, 138, 147,
  151–158, 161, 165, 171–175,
  177–179, 183
Marmalade, 114
Masking tape, 22, 51
Math activities
  birthday, 171–174, 182–184
  hot and sunny day, 48–49, 56–57
  wet and rainy day, 17, 24, 28, 31
  when you have to wait, 116–125
  when you take a walk, 156,
    164–165
  windy day, 68–69
Measurement books, 118
Measuring activities, 28, 48–49, 57,
  116–118, 156
Measuring cups, 28, 47–49, 57, 92,
  183
Measuring spoons, 28, 47–49, 57,
  183
Metal rings, 13
Milk, 183
  jugs, 55
  skim, 49
Milkweed pods, 78
Mirrors, 52, 135, 151, 157
Muffin tins, 55, 93
Multiculturalism, 10, 76, 80–81, 121,
  175
Murals, 19
Music activities, 24, 46
  birthdays, 181–183
  marching, 182
Musical instruments, 17, 24–25, 82,
  127, 182

N
Nametags, 133
National Association for the
  Education of Young Children, 10
National Council of Teachers of
  Mathematics Standards, 117
Neckties, 100
Netting, 39
Newspaper, 35, 51
Newsprint, 13
Number sense, 119–123, 172–173
  candles, 180
Nursery rhymes. *See* Rhymes
Nuts (metal), 91
Nylon stockings, 74

O

Oatmeal boxes, 88
Observation activities
  perfectly beautiful day, 92
  when you take a walk, 151–156,
    161, 164
  windy day, 66–80

P

Paintbrushes, 35, 61, 71, 78, 81, 95,
  97, 166
Paints, 19, 78, 95, 97, 166
  fingerpaint, 97
  watercolors, 35, 81
  white, 71
Paper clips, 68, 158
Paper towels, 97
  tubes, 78, 89, 152
Paper, 12, 19, 28, 30–31, 33, 35–38,
  46, 49, 54–55, 57, 61, 68, 71–75,
  77, 80–81, 125, 135–136, 151–158,
  161, 165–166, 172–173, 175, 177
  airplanes, 77
  bags, 79
  blue, 71
  chart, 45, 48, 62, 69, 79, 92, 111,
    114, 117, 119, 147, 173, 178
  construction, 13, 23, 30, 71, 73, 86,
    94–97, 135–136, 151, 175
  crepe, 185
  cupcake, 96
  cups, 46–49
  fans, 67
  mural, 134
  newsprint, 13, 35, 51
  scraps, 55
  shelf, 97
  shiny, 23, 52, 96–97
  tissue, 51, 78, 89, 185
  waxed, 30
  wrapping, 23, 51, 97, 174
Parquetry blocks, 124
Party games, 185
Paste, 78, 152
Pebbles, 158
Pencils, 98
Pens, 28, 33, 48, 54, 62, 112, 165,
  178
Photographs, 50, 132–134, 179–180
Physical disabilities. *See* Special needs
  children
Piaget, J., 9–10, 190
Pianos, 24–25, 182
Picnic tables, 96
Pie pans, 61, 93
Pill bottles, 158
Pillows, 39, 141

Pin the Tail on the Donkey, 185
Ping-Pong balls, 67
Pins, 158
Pipes, 59
  PVC, 91
Pitchers, 48, 54, 93, 142
Planning skills
  hot and sunny day activities, 44–48,
    50–51
  windy day activities, 75
Planters, 165
Plants, 165
Plastic wrap, 30, 92
Plastic, 30, 56, 96
  bags, 72
  blocks, 30
  bowls, 89
  boxes, 88–89, 93
  bracelets, 90
  fish, 61
  keys, 98
  letters, 61, 111, 178
  milk jugs, 55
  plates, 89, 100
  sheets, 142
  soda bottles, 185
  spools, 89
  squirt bottles, 59–60, 92, 97
  tubs, 60–61
  zippered bags, 79, 183
Plates, 142
  paper, 96
  plastic, 89, 100
Play money, 60, 62, 99
Playdough, 19, 56
Pliers, 91, 96
Poems. *See* Rhymes
Poster board, 132, 171–172,
  179–180, 183, 185
Pots, 61, 100
Potting soil, 165
Potting tools, 165
Poultry basters, 59
Pull toys, 88
Pumpkins, 166
Purses, 99
PVC pipes, 91

Q

Quiet activities
  birthdays, 183
  hot and sunny day, 46, 49, 60,
    62–63
  wet and rainy day, 39–40
  when things go wrong, 142
  when you have to wait, 113,
    115–116
  windy day, 69–70, 76, 80

R

Receipt books, 98–99, 177
Recipes
  frosty chocolate milk, 49
  ice cream, 183–184
  lemonade, 47–48
Reflecting activities
  birthday, 184
  hot and sunny day, 49–51
  windy day, 76, 80
Reggio Emilia schools, 46
Rhymes, 67, 107, 111–116
  "1, 2, 3, 4, 5," 123
  "April Rain Song" by Langston
    Hughes, 36, 188
  "Clouds" by Christina Rosetti, 69
  "The Duel" by Eugene Field, 123
  "The End" by A.A. Milne, 174,
    189
  "Going on a Bear Hunt," 26
  "Hen and Chicks," 107
  "Here Is the Beehive," 107
  "Here's a Ball for Baby," 107
  "In a Spider's Web," 121
  "Jack and Jill," 18, 21
  "Jack Be Nimble," 19, 21
  "The King's Breakfast" by A. A.
    Milne, 114, 189
  "Lemonade Sun" by Rebecca Kai
    Dotlich, 49
  "Milkweed Seeds," 78
  "Mummy Slept Late and Daddy
    Fixed Breakfast" by John Ciardi,
    115
  "My Shadow," by Robert Louis
    Stevenson, 53
  "Quiet Jack," 21
  "Rainy Day," 37
  "Rassberry, Jazzberry,
    Razzmattazzberry, Berry Band"
    by Bruce Degen, 125
  "Rice Pudding," by A. A. Milne,
    114, 189
  "To Bed," 113
  "Wee Willie Winkie," 113
  "The Wind," 74
  books of, 63
Rhythm instruments, 17, 24, 127,
  182
Rhythm sticks, 127, 182
Ribbons, 23, 59, 96
Rice, 158
Rocking chairs, 141
Rope, 51, 153, 156
Rosegrant, T., 10, 190
Rossetti, Christine, 66
Rubber bands, 92

195

Rubber stamps, 177–178
Rugs, 141, 183
Rulers, 28

S

Sailboats, 74
Salt, 55, 158, 183
Sand, 55, 59, 90, 92, 106, 158, 185
Sandboxes, 92, 156
Scales, 92
Scarlet runner beans, 51
Science activities
    for preschoolers, 91–93
    hot and sunny day, 53–62
    perfectly beautiful day, 91–93
    wet and rainy day, 28–34
    when you take a walk, 152, 166
    windy day, 66–74, 78–80
Scissors, 38, 72, 171, 173
Screwdrivers, 91
Seeds, 99
    casings, 78
    catalogs, 99
    sunflower, 50
Seefeldt, C., 10, 12, 14, 73, 160, 190
Shadow tag, 105
Sheets, 39, 51, 95
Shelf paper, 97
Shells, 93
Shoeboxes, 99, 177
Shoes, 158, 179
Shoestrings, 142
Shovels, 59, 90
Sieves, 93
Sifters, 59
Simon Says, 120, 137
Six-pack holders, 59, 97
Skill games
    2-year-olds, 101
    3-year-olds, 101
    4-year-olds, 105–106
    5-year-olds, 105–106
Snacks, 142, 180
    crackers with marmalade, 114
    frosty chocolate milk, 49
    ice cream, 183–184
    lemonade, 47–48
Soap, 60, 97
Social skill builders
    cooperation, 25, 37, 58, 75,
        98–100, 102–104, 120, 126–127
    coping with life events, 145–147
    correcting behaviors, 140–144
    when you take a walk, 163
Socks, 138
Soda bottles, 185
Soil, 34, 61
Songs

"A Tisket, A Tasket," 103
"A You're Adorable," 181
"Charlie Over the Water," 103
"Did You Ever See a Lassie?" 102
"Five Little Speckled Frogs," 122
"Frog in the Middle," 102
"Happy Birthday," 181
"I Love You," 181
"If You're Happy and You Know
    It," 137
"Johnny Works With One
    Hammer," 122
"Let's Take a Walk," 159
"Looby Loo, 103–104
"Love Somebody," 181
"Make New Friends," 135
"Old Man of Peru," 127
"Punchenello," 102
"Ring Around the Rosie," 100
"Round and Round the Village,"
    104
"Running," 101
"Skip to My Lou," 101
"Stars and Stripes Forever," 182
"This Land Is Your Land," 182
"Toodala," 101
"What Will We Do?" 45
"When the Saints Go Marching In,"
    182
"A Young Woman of Leeds," 127
Sousa, John Phillip, 182
Spades, 93
Sparkles, 173
Spatial sense builders, 123–125
Special needs children, 25, 58
    making friends, 139
Sponges, 59–60
Spools, 89
Spoons, 47–48, 59, 61
    measuring, 47–49, 57, 183
    slotted, 61, 93
    wooden, 54
Sprinklers, 62
Squirt bottles, 59–60, 92, 97
Stamps, 177
Staplers, 13, 68, 71, 73, 78, 135–136,
    151, 175, 177
Star stickers, 154, 161
Stethoscopes, 67
Stickers, 52, 154, 161
Sticks, 53, 61
Stones, 61
Stoop tag, 105
Strainers, 58–59, 61
String, 24, 68, 72, 74, 88, 96, 153,
    156
Stuffed animals, 141
Styrofoam peanuts, 96

Sugar, 47–48, 55, 183
Suitcases, 98
Sunflower seeds, 50
Swim suits, 59, 61–62

T

Tables, 39, 52, 67, 91, 97, 127
    coverings, 35, 96
    picnic, 96
Tag board, 13
Tag games, 105
Tambourines, 182
Tank vacuum sweeper, 98
Tape, 23, 52, 78, 95, 132, 134, 152,
    171–172, 174, 177, 179
    duct, 96
    electrical, 22
    masking, 22, 51
    opaque, 158
    two-sided, 185
Telephones, 91, 99–100
Telescopes, 92
Ten-Pins, 185
Tickets, 98–99
Time capsule, 50
Tinker Toys, 91
Tissue paper, 51, 78, 89, 185
Toilet paper tubes, 89
Tool kits, 96, 99–100
Tools, 91, 96, 98
    kitchen, 92
    potting, 165
Toss the ball, 106
Towels, 59
    paper, 97
Transitions, 131
    activities, 132–136
Trash cans, 46, 97
Trays, 54
    sorting, 177
Trees, 50
Triangles, 182
Tricycles, 60, 88
Trowels, 93
Twigs, 61

U

Umbrellas, 53
Unit blocks, 117

V

Van Zupthen, C., 190
Vanilla extract, 183
Velcro, 119
Vygotzky, 10

W

Wading pools, 59, 74
Wallets, 99
Wallpaper, 142
Washcloths, 60
Water table, 59
Water, 30–31, 35, 46–48, 54–59, 61,
    74, 92, 97, 163
Watercolor paints, 35, 81
Watering cans, 61
Wax, 56
Waxed paper, 30
Weights, 72, 74
Wheel toys, 60, 98
Wheels, 53
Wind chimes, 80–81, 160
Wind instruments, 82
Windsocks, 74
Wire, 68, 74
Wolf game, 105
Wood, 56
    blocks, 30
    crates, 100
    letters, 111, 178
    spools, 89
Work boots, 99
Work props, 99
Wrapping paper, 51, 174
    brown, 23, 97

Y

Yarn, 38, 153

198

Creating Readers

Over 1000 Games, Activities, Tongue Twisters, Fingerplays, Songs, and Stories to Get Children Excited about Reading
Pam Schiller

Explore the basic building blocks of reading with *Creating Readers,* the comprehensive resource that develops a strong foundation for pre-readers. *Creating Readers* gives teachers and parents the tools to teach pre-reading skills with more than 1000 games, activities, fingerplays, songs, tongue twisters, poems, and stories for the letters of the alphabet. This valuable resource develops the child's desire to read as well as the skills needed to begin reading. *Creating Readers* starts children ages three to eight toward a future rich with books and reading. 448 pages.

ISBN 0-87659-258-2 / Gryphon House 16375 / Paperback

Available at your favorite bookstore, school supply store, or order from Gryphon House at 800.638.0928 or www.gryphonhouse.com.

Block Play

The Complete Guide to Learning and Playing with Blocks
Sharon MacDonald

Create craft board trees, railroad tracks, and skyscrapers and watch children experience the joy of learning through blocks! Clear descriptions of what children learn by playing with blocks accompany the activities. Each activity is written to take into account the ability and interest level of the children and to encourage developmental skills such as problem solving, math, science, language, and social skills. *Block Play* is a must have for every teacher. 192 pages.

**ISBN 0-87659-253-1
Gryphon House
19327 / Paperback**

ALSO AVAILABLE FROM SHARON MACDONALD
Everyday Discoveries
Squish, Sort, Paint & Build

Wiggle, Giggle & Shake

200 Ways to Move and Learn
Rae Pica

Enhance your classroom with 200 movement-inspiring activities for children ages four to eight. Explore 38 popular classroom themes such as transportation, seasons, health, occupations, holidays, nature, animals, health, and more. This book offers simple, practical, and fun movement activities and ideas grouped according to these popular themes. 192 pages.

**ISBN 0-87659-244-2   Gryphon House
19284 / Paperback**

Available at your favorite bookstore, school supply store, or order from Gryphon House at 800.638.0928 or www.gryphonhouse.com.

Sand and Water Play

Simple, Creative Activities for Young Children
Sherrie West and Amy Cox

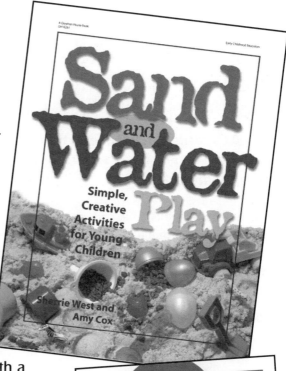

With more than 70 ideas, you'll find new inspiration for your sand and water table with *Sand and Water Play*. Learn creative new ways to invigorate sand and water play in your classroom and encourage problem-solving skills, creativity, fine and gross motor skills, imagination, and social skills. Designed for children ages three to six, *Sand and Water Play* uses fun materials such as bubbles, ice cubes, aquarium rocks, bird seed, mud, rock salt, and others to encourage children's learning while they are having fun. A must for anyone with a sand and water table! 128 pages.

**ISBN 0-87659-247-7 / Gryphon House
16281 / Paperback**

101 Easy, Wacky, Crazy Activities

for Young Children
Carole H. Dibble and Kathy H. Lee

With quick and simple ideas, *101 Easy, Wacky, Crazy Activities* is guaranteed to enliven any day. Try Tongue Painting (yes, Tongue Painting!) or Squishy Squeezy (a clean and messy activity!) and open the door to creative discovery. Encourage children to think creatively, problem solve, and have fun while learning. Written by two experienced teachers, this collection of open-ended ideas is a book teachers and parents will want to keep handy. 144 pages. 2000.

ISBN 0-87659-207-8 / Gryphon House / 18642 / Paperback

**Available at your favorite bookstore, school supply store,
or order from Gryphon House at 800.638.0928 or www.gryphonhouse.com.**

201

The Giant Encyclopedia of Circle Time and Group Activities for Children 3 to 6

Over 600 Favorite Circle Time Activities Created by Teachers for Teachers
Edited by Kathy Charner

Open to any page in this book and you will find an activity for circle or group time written by an experienced teacher. Filled with over 600 activities covering 48 themes, this book is jam-packed with ideas that were tested by teachers in the classroom. 510 pages.

**ISBN 0-87659-181-0 / Gryphon House
16413 / Paperback**

The Giant Encyclopedia of Theme Activities for Children 2 to 5

Over 600 Favorite Activities Created by Teachers for Teachers
Edited by Kathy Charner

This popular potpourri of over 600 classroom-tested activities actively engages children's imaginations and provides many months of learning fun. Organized into 48 popular themes, from Dinosaurs to Circuses to Outer Space, these favorites are the result of a nationwide competition. 511 pages.

**ISBN 0-87659-166-7 / Gryphon House
19216 / Paperback**

Available at your favorite bookstore, school supply store, or order from Gryphon House at 800.638.0928 or www.gryphonhouse.com.

500 Five Minute Games

Quick and Easy Activities for 3 to 6 Year Olds
Jackie Silberg

Enjoy five minute games that are easy, fun, and developmentally appropriate. Children unwind, communicate, and build self-esteem as they have fun. Each game indicates the particular skill developed. 272 pages.

"...Your young class will be so involved in meaningful learning that the wiggles will disappear."
—Texas Child Care

ISBN 0-87659-172-1 / Gryphon House / 16455 / Paperback

Transition Tips and Tricks

For Teachers
Jean Feldman

The author of the best-selling book *Transition Time* brings you more attention-grabbing, creative activities that provide children with an outlet for wiggles, while giving their brains a jump start with cross-lateral movement games. Catch their attention with songs, games, and fingerplays for any time of the day. These classroom-tested ideas are sure to become favorites! 216 pages.

**ISBN 0-87659-216-7 / Gryphon House
16728 / Paperback**

**Available at your favorite bookstore, school supply store,
or order from Gryphon House at 800.638.0928 or www.gryphonhouse.com.**

Linking Language

Simple Language and Literacy Activities Throughout the Curriculum

Robert Rockwell, Debra Hoge, and Bill Searcy

Filled with practical, everyday activities to build language development and early literacy into your daily schedule. Use during circle time, snack time, dramatic play, or any time throughout the day to develop children's language skills. The authors discuss both expressive language (talking), and receptive language (listening), as well as the beginnings of reading and writing. Each cross-curricular activity includes ways to enhance children's vocabularies, questions to help the teacher evaluate children's progress, an annotated list of books that relate to the activity, and age-appropriate suggestions for writing experiences. 227 pages.

**ISBN 0-87659-202-7 / Gryphon House
17561 / Paperback**

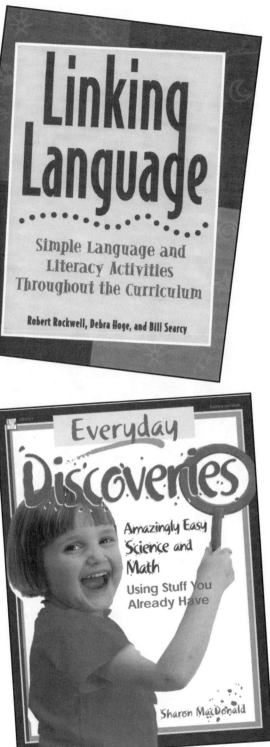

Everyday Discoveries

Amazingly Easy Science and Math Using Stuff You Already Have

Sharon MacDonald

Science and math concepts are embedded in the things children do every day. With this book, children learn the how, the why, and the what happens next with these open-ended, self-directed activities. *Everyday Discoveries* shows how easily and naturally children can learn science and math in preschool programs, early primary classrooms, child care centers, and home care settings. 245 pages.

**ISBN 0-87659-196-9 / Gryphon House
18117 / Paperback**

206

The Inclusive Early Childhood Classroom

Easy Ways to Adapt Learning Centers for All Children

Patti Gould and Joyce Sullivan

All children require nurturing and stimulating learning environments, but many typical early childhood classrooms should be modified for children with special needs. *The Inclusive Early Childhood Classroom* is written to help teachers look at classroom design in a new way and to suggest different ways of approaching activities so children with special needs can be successful. By modifying the classroom and activities, all children will be actively engaged. Each chapter focuses on either a learning center, such as art or science, or a time of the day, such as snack time or dismissal, with particular attention to the needs of children who are developmentally delayed, orthopedically impaired, have Autism/Pervasive Developmental Disorder, Attention Deficit Hyperactivity Disorder, behavorial issues, motor planning problems, or visual impairments. 208 pages.

ISBN 0-87659-203-5 / Gryphon House 19652 / Paperback

Early Learning Environments That Work

Rebecca Isbell and Betty Exelby

The classroom environment is a vital part of a child's learning experience. *Early Learning Environments That Work* explores how you can work with furniture, color, materials, storage, lighting, and more

to encourage learning through classroom arrangement. Each chapter gives you detailed illustrations and photographs to help you set up or arrange what you already have in the classroom.

Early Learning Environments that Work is an innovative guide for teachers who want to make the most of their classroom environment. Transform your classroom into a beautiful and meaningful space that will stimulate the development of young children while providing adults with a great place to work. 192 pages.

"This will be one of the essential books on the early educator's shelf." **—Gwen Morgan, Wheelock College**

**ISBN 0-87659-256-6 / Gryphon House
14387 / Paperback**